DON'T PUT lipstick on the CAT

HUMOROUS TALES OF MOTHERHOOD

D1710542

KERSTEN CAMPBELL

PLAIN SIGHT PUBLISHING
AN IMPRINT OF CEDAR FORT, INC.
SPRINGVILLE, UTAH

ISBN 13: 978-1-4621-1557-0

Published by Plain Sight Publishing, an imprint of Cedar Fort, Inc.,
2373 W. 700 S., Springville, UT 84663
Distributed by Cedar Fort, Inc., www.cedarfort.com

LIBRARY OF CONGRESS CATALOGING-IN-PUBLICATION DATA
Campbell, Kersten, 1970- author.
Don't put lipstick on the cat / Kersten Campbell.
    pages cm
Collection of humorous stories about the author's family.
ISBN 978-1-4621-1557-0
1. Families--Humor. 2. Mormon families--Humor. I. Title.
PN6231.F3C36 2015
818'.602--dc23
                          2014049712

Cover design by Angela Baxter
Cover design © 2015 by Lyle Mortimer
Edited and typeset by Eileen Leavitt

Printed in the United States of America

10 9 8 7 6 5 4 3 2 1

Contents

To my family, who is everything to me.
May we continue to have many hilarious times together.

THIS DIARY BELONGS TO:

Kersten Campbell: An extremely enthusiastic housewife who tries hard but is terrible at housekeeping. The following are members of her family and make various appearances in the family stories.

Grizz: Kersten's husband. The opposite of her in every single way.

Violet: Teenager known for her dramatic mood swings.

Scoot: Ten-year-old troublemaker of the family. His curiosity gets him into serious scrapes, but somehow he is always able to "scoot" out of trouble.

Birdie: Doesn't really exist in the real world. Eight years old and extremely creative, she loves to invent things that leave the rest of the family dazed and baffled.

Hazel: The five-year-old tattletale of the family. Practically perfect in every way. Very stubborn. Never gives up. Truthful to a fault. Says embarrassing things to people in the grocery store.

Moo: The three-year-old baby. Very picky-eater. Drinks truckloads of milk and doesn't eat much else. Also known as "Super Moo" because of his fanatical love of super heroes. Unwittingly causes nuclear disasters all over the house.

1

A Cinderella Story

YOU KNOW IT'S TIME FOR A DATE NIGHT WHEN THE BEST TIME ALONE YOU and your husband can recall is yesterday morning when you locked the bathroom door against angry little fists so you could bond with each other while flossing your teeth. This was the sad state of affairs in my household when Birdie came up with a grand scheme to save our marriage.

"Mom, isn't being married to a handsome man so romantic?" she asked, watching me work on getting Moo dressed. Her eyes stared dreamily up at me.

"Yup," I said, plugging my nose and holding up a dirty diaper. "Pure romance."

"Humph," said Violet. "He may be handsome, but he sure is bossy—telling me what to do all the time. You should've been more careful and picked out someone less opinionated. Then he wouldn't conflict so much with my personality."

"Really?" I said, handing her the dirty diaper and directing her to the outside garbage can.

On her way out the door, she added, "Come to think of it, you're bossy too. Maybe I was wrong. Maybe you were made for each other."

"Made for each other," sighed Birdie as I herded everyone into the laundry room. "Do you think I'll ever find someone like that when I

1

grow up?" Then she grinned. "I want to have an exciting marriage like you and Daddy."

There was a loud crash in the kitchen. "Don't worry," yelled my son. "I was practicing juggling with the milk jugs. I'll clean it up."

I peered at my daughters over the mountain of socks at the foot of the dryer. "I could do with a little less excitement," I said. "Besides, life isn't all excitement and romance. There's a lot of hard work involved in a marriage."

"What do you mean?" asked Violet, coming in from the garage. "I do most of the work around here. All you guys have to do is make googly eyes at each other."

"Really?" I said, handing her a pile of clothes and directing her to put them away.

"See what I mean?" she said. "Work, work, work, all day long." Then she stomped off to the bedrooms. "You should've named me Cinderella," she called over her shoulder.

"Gosh," I said, grinning at my eight-year-old. "Romance and a wicked stepmother. Now all we need is a royal ball."

"That's it!" shouted Birdie.

"That's what?"

"A royal ball. That's just what you and Daddy need to get more romance in your life and save your marriage."

"Huh?"

"Don't you worry about a thing," she said. "I'm going to give you a night you'll never forget." Then she ran off to find her brother.

That night when my husband walked in the door, he got a big surprise.

"What in the world?" he asked as he set down his computer case.

"Don't say a word," I said, blowing a gigantic feather out of my eyes. "She made me do it." I pointed at my eight-year-old.

"You're wearing your old prom dress? How did you ever . . . ?"

"Fit into it?" I finished his sentence, adjusting the ridiculous-looking dress-up hat adorned with poofy feathers that my daughter had forced me to wear.

"That's why she's wearing a superman cape," said my daughter. "To cover up the bare spots in the back."

My husband grinned. "Brilliant!"

I glared. "How come he doesn't have to dress up?"

We were interrupted by my son, who had dressed up in his father's Sunday suit. "Sir? Madam? If you would step this way?" His sleeves drooped over his fingers as he pointed to the kitchen. "Dinner is served."

My husband took my arm and said, "That's quite the lipstick you've got on there."

"That's because it was applied by a three-year-old," I replied with my clown lips, jerking my thumb in my daughter's direction. "Another one of her ideas."

My daughter smiled and patted the head of our toddler. "He wanted to help," she said.

Moo pointed up at me. "You look funny," he said.

My husband snorted, and I elbowed him in the ribs. We were seated by my son and treated to two elegant bowls of chocolate chip soup.

"Dad's has milk in it," my daughter whispered to me. "But I made yours with Slimfast because of the trouble we had with the dress."

"Gee, thanks," I said.

Suddenly our dinner was interrupted by an unearthly screeching noise.

"That's your dinner music," said my son.

Violet walked in, sawing on her violin. *Squeak, squeak, squaaaaak.* We were being treated to a fine rendition of "Row, Row, Row Your Boat," the only song she had ever learned.

"Care to dance?" asked my husband over the top of the scraping and groaning and rasping of the violin. Grinning, he held out his hand.

"Why not?" I said, adjusting my superman cape and flipping my feathers back.

We stepped onto the living room dance floor, twirling, and whirling to the screeching and moaning of the violin, until we realized the moaning was my daughter singing:

"Work, work, work your daughter—work her to the bone . . ."

"I want to dance too!" said Moo, burrowing in between our bodies and latching on to my husband's legs.

"Me too!" said Hazel, pulling on my superman cape. And so we danced, my husband thumping around with a kid barnacle on his foot and me with a kindergartner riding piggyback. Birdie did cartwheels around us, while my son juggled spaghetti squash to the music.

It was a royal ball to remember. And in the midst of it all, my husband leaned over and kissed my clown lips, and my heart swelled with love for my handsome prince. All was right with the world, and as we made googly eyes at each other in between dodging spaghetti squash and twirling our kids in the air, I knew I wouldn't trade a romantic night like this for anything.

2

Yo Ho! Mow the Man Down

IT WAS THE YEAR OF THE LAWNMOWER MAN. OR AT LEAST IT WAS THE YEAR I was finally going to get one. A little one, at least. I could hardly wait. My son had turned ten—the magical age when my husband had promised to finally pass the sacred lawn-mowing torch down to the next generation. Finally, there would be someone to keep the lawn trimmed when my husband went on his long business trips. Scoot had been looking forward to this event for nearly eleven years. My husband had made sure of that. He, who had taken upon himself the devout guardianship of the 37,987 or so blades of grass surrounding our ranch-style dwelling, had been building up each child's enthusiasm for this great responsibility since the day he or she was born.

"You should never mow the same way twice," he would whisper to the newborn baby as the doctors worked on stitching me up from the birth. "You can get ruts in your lawn. And watch out for crabgrass!" he would shout, eyes wide, scaring the baby with his intensity. Then, when the baby would cry, he would feel bad for scaring the child and whisper words of comfort. "There, there. It scares me too. But don't worry. They've got preemergent herbicides that'll take care of just about anything."

And so, it was with great anticipation that my son waited for his tenth birthday—the day he would be ready to take over the hallowed responsibility of caring for the painstakingly tended sea of emerald in our front yard. Even more important—his first chance to legitimately wield a power tool. (We won't talk about previous illegitimate power tool wielding attempts).

Unfortunately, as with all highly anticipated events, we ran into a little problem.

"Honey," said my husband over the phone when the day finally arrived. His voice sounded desperate. "I've got a late meeting. I won't be able to come home in time to teach our son to mow the lawn. He was so looking forward to it."

"No problem," I said, flinging clean dishes from the dishwasher into the cupboard. "You don't have to worry. I'll just get out old Mr. Ugly and teach him myself." Mr. Ugly was the giant, loud, ancient, cantankerous lawn mower passed down to us from the previous owner of our house. My husband had a strange attachment to the grumpy old power tool, despite its reluctance to do such things as start and move forward. Whenever I teased him about it, his reply was that we couldn't buy a new one lest we offend the lawn and lose some of our good turf-growing karma.

"I don't know . . . ," my husband hesitated. "Have you ever mowed a lawn before?"

"Tons of times! Well, I've cut the boys' hair often enough with the clippers. The same principles apply, right?" I said, throwing a plastic lid like a Frisbee into a drawer across the room.

"What do you mean, the same principles apply?" asked my husband, his voice suddenly tight.

There was a thunderous crash when I missed the drawer and sent the lid flying into the glassware cupboard.

"What was that?" asked my husband, an octave higher than usual.

"Oops. You silly kids," I said to my youngest two children who came in to see what all the noise was about. They gave me a confused stare. "I've gotta go," I said over the choking noise of my husband's protests. "The kids need me. I'll let you know how it goes."

Late that afternoon, my son and I found ourselves staring down Mr. Ugly in the middle of the driveway. It stared back at us with its seedy chipped red paint and its gaping jaw. The curved metal in front was bent upwards in a menacing sneer from a previous argument with a giant cherry tree, and one of the cutting blades stuck out from under it like a wicked front tooth.

"Do you know how to start it?" I asked my son, whispering so as not to disturb Mr. Ugly's peaceful slumber.

He looked at me. "You're supposed to know how to start it. You're the one teaching me, remember?"

"I do, I do," I said after clearing my throat a few times. "If there's one thing I know about, it's how to start a silly lawn mower." Gingerly, I tiptoed close enough to lean down and reach the pull-starter. I pulled back hard, and Mr. Ugly belched a great ball of thick black smoke and tried to jerk my arm out of its socket before I could release the cord, as if he had been offended by my remarks. Then he was silent. This process was repeated twelve more times before my son finally interrupted.

"Dad pushes that red button forty-six times before he pulls the string," he said.

"I knew that," I said, rubbing my shoulder. "I was just testing your memory. How come it took you so long to remember?" I made my son push the red button eighty-nine times just for good measure, and this time, when I pulled on the starter, Mr. Ugly roared to life with a thunderous bang that sounded like gunfire, sending Harold, our neighbor who was trimming his roses, diving behind a forsythia bush for cover.

My son's eyes lit up at this display of raw power. "When can I do it? Can I push it now?" he begged.

"Only after," I said, "I give you some professional lawn-mowing tips. Now, the great thing is Mr. Ugly is one of the first of the self-propelled lawn mowers. You just push down on this handle and . . ." With a great lurch and surprising agility for an old man, Mr. Ugly took off toward the street, yanking my feet out from underneath me and dragging me behind. A startled jogger began to sprint as he saw us coming for him down the steep hill that led to the main road. With sheer brute strength, I managed to skid behind Mr. Ugly as he mowed through a raspberry patch and over the top of someone's privet hedge. Then, perhaps hearing the insults yelled at him by our fussy neighbor, Harold, Mr. Ugly swung left and mowed straight for the trembling forsythia bush, sending flying projectiles in Harold's direction as it deliberately gobbled up rocks, tree roots, and small toys in its path. Covering his head with his arms, Harold ran screaming into his house. But there was no need for panic, because Mr. Ugly's progress was suddenly halted by the same giant cherry tree that had given him his first ugly scars.

My son loped over to me from the driveway. "Dad says you've got to show Mr. Ugly who's boss," he said, peeling my remains from the foot of the tree.

"That's just what I was doing," I said, pulling a twig out from between my front teeth, "by steering him into the cherry tree."

Using wisdom gleaned from my vast experience of five minutes with the lawn mower, I suddenly decided that the best way to teach my son would be to coach him from the safety of the front porch. I handed over Mr. Ugly and retreated to the sidelines. I tried to think of my most sage lawn-mowing wisdom.

"Don't be boring and mow everything the same height!" I yelled at him over Mr. Ugly's roar. "Be bold! Make some designs as you go. Stripes would be pretty, don't you think?"

Just then my husband walked up. "My lawn!" he cried. "What have you done to my beautiful lawn?"

I looked out over the expanse of mutilated tree roots and chewed-up yard toys and the great bald spot leading up to the new slashes in the trunk of the cherry tree, and I repeated the age-old wisdom that every mother tells her child after a particularly bad haircut.

"Don't worry. Just give it a few weeks. It'll grow out."

3

How to Survive a Family Reunion

WHAT DO YOU GET WHEN YOU HAVE NINE CHILDREN AND THIRTY-NINE grandchildren? One heck of a reunion party—even if, after last year, some of the grandchildren were hauled away to police headquarters for questioning about a suspicious fire in a neighboring farmer's alfalfa field. That and another unfortunate incident involving a potato cannon and an injured cow is why this year's reunion committee decided that there must be some means of maintaining order in the chaos.

"Our children are not juvenile delinquents," said my sister-in-law Sue. "They just happen to be more inquisitive and resourceful than most other children." Then she looked around, giving us all a hooded Yoda-like stare. "We must teach them to channel their powers for good."

My husband piped up, "What about a reward system, where we give them prizes for doing jobs and taking care of the little kids?"

"What? You mean *bribe* our own children?" cried my nervous sister-in-law.

Good for you, Sue, I thought. I felt comforted by the fact that someone was going to stand up for what was morally right.

Sue chewed her fingernails thoughtfully. "Sounds great to me," she said, nodding her head.

Everyone around the table nodded in enthusiastic agreement, and so Reunion Tokens were born: a reward system whereby children could earn plastic coins for things like "not following through on their idea to stuff a snake down their younger cousin's T-shirt" and other such golden behaviors. At the end of the day, the children would be able to squander their wealth at a reunion store filled with shining and wondrous breakable, shoddily-made, plastic plunder.

The first day of the reunion proved that the system worked like magic. What a difference from the last reunion! Kids ran around like mad asking for jobs, reading to younger cousins, holding babies, making cookies for the adults, and in general, staying out of jail.

My own son, I noticed, was quite the young capitalist. He wiped the table seven different times for seven different people, and when the aunts and uncles finally caught on to his scheme, he ran around offering to finish other cousins' work for an exorbitant fee.

Then in the evening, when the reunion store opened, he would buy all of the Smarties and sell them the next day for profit.

In spite of his questionable focus on worldly treasure, I was proud of him for showing initiative.

"I have to admit," I told my husband later that night. "I had my doubts about your reward system, but it seems to be working. The kids are learning hard work and responsibility."

He nodded smugly before he went to sleep.

It was only on the fourth day that I started to see that my doubts may have been founded after all when I noticed my son seemed to have taken over the reunion store. He had bought the store out with his amassed token fortune and was now instructing underling cousins on how to deal Smarties on the street.

"I get half of everything you take," he told them. "And don't let anyone disrespect the family, you hear? Now get outta here and go make me some dough." He dismissed them with a wave of his hand, and they all scrambled away.

Was I only imagining that he had developed a Godfather-like accent overnight? That night I saw him in his bed, counting tokens and grinning to himself, his braces glinting wickedly under the fluorescent bulbs.

The next day, my son was confronted by an irate uncle. "I never thought I'd see the day where a nephew of mine would be involved in taking candy from a baby," he said, holding his crying two-year-old girl.

My son shrugged. "She didn't have protection from the Family. She was refusing to pay up. Thus I couldn't protect her from other criminals and malicious thieves."

My brother-in-law shook his fist, "I'll tell you who's a malicious thief, you little—"

"Okay, that's it!" I cried, taking my son by the collar and turning him upside down over my knee so that I could shake all the tokens out of his pockets.

"Mom, Mom! Don't! Quit it! It was just a joke . . ."

Then I dragged him into his bedroom and bankrupted his little token empire in one fell swoop.

Sheesh. Kids. You try to teach them hard work and responsibility, and all they do is turn your system into a criminal enterprise. I shook my head and stared at his bag of tokens. Really. I ask you. Where in the world did my son ever learn to act like a Mafia boss?

I looked over my shoulder at my brother-in-law comforting his daughter and glaring at my son. *Good grief, it was only a pack of Smarties,* I thought, annoyed at his coddling parental behavior. Maybe I'd have to "off" him for disrespecting my family. It'd take him weeks to get unstuck from the swirly slide. Suddenly, an evil grin stole across my face. I looked down, shaking my son's bag of plunder, feeling the pleasing weight of it in my hands, and I wondered just how many tokens it would take to hire a nephew underling to do the job for me.

4

Ra! Ra! Roo! Kick 'Em in the Shoe!

WHEN YOU'RE THE ONLY ONE IN YOUR FAMILY WHO DOESN'T UNDERSTAND SPORTS, life can get a little lonely on game nights. This is why I found myself volunteering to go to a college basketball game with my family one bleak, wintry night during dinner. I couldn't stand the thought of another three hours alone with the shopping channel.

"*You're* coming to the game with us?" asked my teenage daughter, Violet, her hand on her hip, giving me her best teenage lip curl.

"You don't have to sound so surprised," I replied, dishing her some salad. "Moms can go to basketball games too."

"But, Mom," she said, "you *hate* sports. You said you thought competition was for overly macho, immature men who felt like they had to prove something."

My husband choked on his lettuce and then winced. He was still nursing a rib injury from church basketball, a ruthless tradition that transforms fine upstanding gentlemen who are a smidge past their prime into vicious cannibals with bones through their noses and very sharp elbows.

I cleared my throat. "With the exception of you, of course, dear," I soothed. "Besides, I don't hate competition. I've competed before."

My three oldest children laughed. "You?" asked my son. "Like when?"

I tapped my chin with the salad tongs. "Let's see. I once won a yodeling contest on the playground in second grade. It was just after we watched *The Sound of Music*. I had been practicing hard with my poodle, Aber Crombie Terwiliger, at home. I thought it was fun to see how many times I could yodel before he would run and hide under the bed."

My son laughed. "Yodeling? You call that a sport?"

I straightened. "Okay, how about in drivers ed when I edged out Spud Wilson in the parallel parking contest with my thirty-second Y-turn maneuver."

"Drivers ed?" wheezed Violet between her bursts of laughter. "What kind of a competition is that?"

"What?" I said, lifting my chin. "Parallel parking is an extreme sport. You need to have very athletic neck-turning muscles. It takes talent."

I sighed amid the guffaws. Was there no respect for greatness? I decided I would show them what an impressive sports fan I could be.

We settled down in our seats, and after taking one look at the agitated spectators, I began to dig through my purse.

"Mom, what are you doing? The game is starting," said Violet.

I scoured deeper, poking my head into the bag. "I'm looking for wet wipes. Somebody's got to tell that boy over there that that he's got frosting all over his chin. He must've had a birthday party or something before the game."

"Mom," my daughter said, moaning, "that's not frosting. It's our school colors. We're crimson and gray, remember?"

Oh. I snapped my purse shut just in time for the shark hand clap. A whole stadium full of Jaws. Very scary. Well, when in Rome, do as the Romans do.

I stuck three fingers on top of my head and began to make loud, fearful hissing noises. Hey, this was starting to be fun. I was so menacing that I scared away all of the sharks around me. The man sitting next to me scooted over one seat.

My daughter yanked my arm down. "Mom. What are you doing?" she hissed. "You're supposed to clap your hands like a shark."

"I'm an iguana," I replied. "My old school mascot. It was this huge reptile dressed in lederhosen. Way scarier than a shark. Have you seen the spikes on those things?"

She blinked. "What town did you say you grew up in?"

"Ithaca, Wisconsin. It wasn't really a town, per se, more of a populated area."

"Uh-huh," she said. "Ithaca Iguanas. Way scary. Just don't do it anymore, okay?"

I looked at her. "Does this mean you don't want me to do my prize-winning yodel when they score?"

Her eyes widened in horror.

I nodded. Fine. I could try to fit in with the crowd. I noticed a lot of fans yelling things at the players on the court. One of the red jerseys missed a free throw.

"Hey, eighty-nine, get some glasses!" I shouted.

People stared. My daughter slouched down in her seat and put the hood of her sweatshirt up. My husband reached over and patted my knee. "That's one of our players, hon. We like to cheer for those guys."

I sighed and headed for the concession stand. I guess sporting events do teach a very valuable lesson. Stick to the things you know about: like eating nachos until you're sick. Now there's a competition I can win. Don't mess with me, bad boy! *Hisssssssssssss.*

5

Snow Days

WINTER IS THAT BEAUTIFUL TIME OF YEAR WHEN SNOWFLAKES BLANKET THE earth in peaceful splendor, frosted panes glisten in the morning light, and all great men and women raise their arms in the air and say, "Boy, these arms feel like gelatin from shoveling so much. I sure wish it would stop snowing." This was what I found myself saying one year when my husband was out of town, and I was faced with ten inches of snow in my driveway. "A snow day! We're snowed in!" chanted my children, jumping up and down at the window.

I groaned. This is because a snow day is to child mischief as raw hot dogs are to a pregnant lady. Snow days feed mischief, making it grow and spread like a cancer until, eventually, after the initial excitement of a snow day wears off, the children are all struck with the dreaded "Cabin Fever," which causes them to develop a sudden fever for scientific experiments with such items as my new blender, a paper clip, and their little baby brother.

It was only moments before that I found myself putting the kibosh on one such exploration into the world of science.

"No, it's not a snowman," whispered my son, Scoot, to his younger sister. "It's a snow*Dan*." He rubbed his hands together as he continued to explain. "We'll just grab Dan, the neighbor's cat, and roll him up into a great big snowball with only his head sticking out—"

"Okay, that's it," I interrupted, lifting my son up by the collar. "I think it's time for you to come outside and help me shovel the snow from the driveway."

"Aw, Mom. I can't shovel. I have a bump on my toe," he whined. "I can't walk, see? Last week I couldn't even kick a soccer ball at my best friend." He limped around the living room with intense sound effects.

I frowned. "Don't you mean kick a soccer ball *to* your best friend?"

He shook his head. "Naw. We don't have nets at school, so we kick the ball as hard as we can at each other. It's fun."

I had closed my eyes for a moment and was trying to process this information when I was suddenly struck with a brilliant idea. Why break your back shoveling snow for hours and hours when you have a perfectly good piece of power equipment in your garage that can do the job for you?

Minutes later I was revving up the car engine. I waved at the children with their noses pressed up against the window, and I backed the car up slowly over the snow, hitting the brake as I reached the street. Then I waved again, shifted gears, and pulled the car forward. Back and forth, back and forth until, presto! Ten inches of snow was now compacted into a smooth, glossy, entry way to the garage. No shoveling required! And no more tromping through snow up to your knees to get to the mailbox. I briefly considered doing the sidewalk, but then thought better of it.

I stared at my neighbor's driveway. I bet he could use a little help too. In fact, this was so easy I could do all the neighbors' driveways!

Afterward, I came into the house whistling. Nothing like a good deed to cheer yourself up in the morning. I had to stop mid-whistle, however, when several kids whizzed by me, chasing Moo with a fish net.

"He's a bumblebee. We're trying to catch him," they squealed.

My eyes narrowed. There was something different about that chubby little bumblebee. He looked a bit too . . . colorful. I scooped him up as he scampered past for the third time.

"What in the world? I thought you were supposed to be babysitting," I said to Violet.

She pouted. "I was!"

"Then why, may I ask, does your little brother's face look like a rainbow trout?" I looked down at my youngest son. He blinked up at me through eyelashes painted with mascara, and there were fifteen different colors and variations of makeup all over his face. Then he popped a thumb painted with shiny red nail polish into his mouth.

My daughter shrugged. "I decided that since he and I had the same skin tone, I could see what colors would look good on me."

The phone rang. Sighing, I ran to pick it up.

Me: "Well, good morning, Hilary."

Hilary: "Have you looked outside your window this morning? Some wise guy came and drove all over our driveways before we could get out to shovel, and now it's slicker than an iceberg out there. Did you see or hear anything unusual when you woke up?"

Me: "Um. Er . . . no."

Hilary: "And that's not the worst of it. I sent Harold off to work this morning, and since our driveway is on an incline, the car shot down the driveway and out into the street like he was riding the luge in the Winter Olympics. He's lucky to be alive."

Me (trying to avoid the topic of seeing anything unusual): "Hey, you've always wanted Harold to develop a talent. Maybe this could be his new thing. When is the next Winter Olympics anyway?"

I hung up the phone. Another good deed gone bad. But there was no time to worry about that. I had to go hide all of the paper clips. I thought I heard the blender in the living room.

6

Rub-a-Dub-Dub, Six Kids in a Tub

WHEN YOU ARE A MOTHER IN CHARGE OF A FAMILY, EVERY DAY IS FRAUGHT with perilous dilemmas and burning questions that only you, through your amazing wit and marvelous ingenuity have the wisdom to solve. You, as a mother, are required to crack mysteries and solve riddles that are so tough, so astounding, and so mind boggling, they would catapult even the most exceptional detective mind into everlasting lunacy. No amateur mind could solve riddles such as these startling questions you face every day: How did your husband's underwear get in the freezer? Who stuck the spaghetti all over the cat? What happened to the Thanksgiving turkey that was sitting on the table a few minutes ago? If your son didn't go to the bathroom in the potty, where did he go to the bathroom? And last but not least, how in the world can you get ten children bathed, brushed, and ready for church in less than ten minutes? This was the burning question facing me during a visit to my sister-in-law's house after we woke up late one Sunday morning.

"What are we going to do?" screeched my sister-in-law Sue, cracking her knuckles and pacing in front of the clock. "I've only got one bathroom."

My sister-in-law is your basic nervous person. This is unfortunate because I am allergic to nervous people. The allergic reaction I have doesn't make me sneeze, it makes me suddenly calm, as if nothing in the world matters, especially not being late for church. The more nervous my sister-in-law became, the slower my heart beat until I had to check my breathing to make sure I was still alive.

"Don't worry," I said with confidence. "I've got the perfect solution. Let's do a cousin bath assembly line."

Another one of my reactions to nervous people is that I suddenly become even more brilliant at solving mysteries and coming up with insane solutions to their problems. This does not help to calm their nervous sensibilities.

"An assembly line?" she said in an agitated voice, biting her nails.

"Yeah. Ford Motor Company does it. Why can't we?" I asked, serenely. I explained how we could set up a sort of "kid car wash" with her at one end of the bathtub and me at the other.

She frowned. "I don't know. These are kids, not cars."

"Peee-shaw!" I said, unruffled. "Kids . . . cars—what's the difference?"

I, being your basic devious person, decided to trick the six youngest children into the tub with a mountainous pile of bubbles. I knew it was going to be a easy sell when there was an earth-shaking stampede and tornado of flying clothes on the way to the tub.

After the dust settled, and a volcano of bubbles erupted from the tub, we rolled up our sleeves and reached blindly through the suds in order to find the children. We soon learned what the difference was between cars and kids. For one thing, kids are not inanimate objects, to be "washed and waxed" at will.

"Hey, you!" I yelled to one of the four-year-olds. "Get back here. I want to soap behind your ears." I was having trouble deciphering which kid was which after they had all donned bubble wigs and beards. All I could hear was a splash and a giggle as their soapy bodies slithered out of my grasp whenever I tried to catch one.

"Where's the baby? I just had him," cried my sister-in-law when she grabbed his foot and he shot across the tub.

"Don't worry! I've got him," yelled Hazel, catching the flopping little fish of a boy. It was then that I noticed Hazel still had all her clothes on.

"Hey, son, where are you going?" I asked three-year-old Moo.

"I've got to go to the bathroom," he answered, drenching me with a tidal wave as he climbed out of the antique claw-foot tub and over the top of my head in order to convey himself to the proper facilities. I tried to stand up to find a towel, and the next thing I knew, my head was underwater, bobbing for rubber duckies.

"Are you okay?" asked my sister-in-law in the fuzzy way you hear voices under the water.

I brought my head up and stared at her through a watery mist. "You might want to take the shampoo away from the kids. The floor is getting a tad slippery over here."

"No!" yelled my daughter as I scrambled back up to my feet. "*I'm* washing Jenny's hair."

My sister-in-law and I looked at two-year-old Jenny. Her hair had been styled with fourteen shampoo spikes sticking out in all directions. She was yelling too, but instead of sound, a huge bubble emerged out of her open mouth. After that, we couldn't see much except a cyclone of arms and legs protruding from the bubble mountain, which grew bigger and bigger from all the agitation of the water until it just about reached the ceiling.

"Okay, that's it," said my sister-in-law, her nervous disposition suddenly gone. "We need to take charge here." She reached inside the monstrous mass of bubbles and marshaled the kids in a line, soaped all their nooks and crannies, and slid them over to me for shampooing.

At one point I found myself shampooing a turtle. "What's this?" I cried.

"Swifty wanted a bath too," replied two little eyes, blinking at me through a hole in the bubbles. "It gets dusty under the stereo speaker."

I stared at my sister-in-law. "There's a turtle living under your stereo speaker?"

She shrugged with an uncharacteristic nonchalance. "He's happy there."

In the face of her surprising tranquility my peaceful world began to crumble. I wondered if the five-minute rule applied to creatures in bathtubs. Anything in the water for less than five minutes couldn't possibly have time to leave anything undesirable in the tub, right?

I looked at the changing color of the water next to Jenny. Oops. I could be wrong about that. But there was no time to worry about that problem. My new calm partner and I had to move on to our next challenging question: how many bagels with cream cheese can you sneak into the front row of church without attracting too much attention to yourself? Answer: not many, if your husband catches you first. See? We moms can crack any riddle. We're professionals.

7

The Patriotic Diet

IF IT'S TRUE THAT YOU ARE WHAT YOU EAT, THEN I WOULD BE A 160-POUND chocolate doughnut. I would have a cheesecake head, french fry arms, and potato chip feet. I can't help it. I love to eat junk food.

Every morning, I wake up and think to myself, *Will it be bran flakes and Metamucil . . . or Belgian waffles topped with a truckload of syrup and whipped cream?* Well, it's no contest. Since I'm definitely trying for an overall healthy lifestyle, it's the bran flakes . . . sprinkled on top of the mound of cream on top of the waffle.

Until this morning I wondered if it was really such a crime to serve a whole box of mint chip ice cream with seven spoons at family dinner. Think of the calcium being consumed. Why, if every family upheld this beloved family tradition, osteoporosis would be virtually wiped from the face of the earth! Once again, my family's quirkiness had the potential to rid the world of a great scourge.

But then, this morning, Hazel followed me into the bathroom. "Mom? Why is your belly so big? It's way bigger than mine," she said.

My shaving husband choked down a laugh.

I glared at him. "It means I'm smart," I said. "When there's no more room for ideas in my brain, they just congregate elsewhere."

My daughter pointed at my stomach. "Then you must be really smart," she said.

This time my husband laughed out loud. I followed him into the bedroom and tried to force my pants to button. Oh man! I should have done my bicep curls yesterday. I sucked in my stomach. There. That was better. Slowly, I let my breath out and turned toward my husband.

"What the?" he yelled, when the button popped off my pants and shot toward his eye like a bullet from his thirty-aught-six. He fell into a crumpled heap on the bed.

Oops. I guess it was *way* past time to go on a diet. Don't get me wrong. I love diets—especially the ones that I invent. Like the time I invented the "Add-a-letter" diet, where every day you change the first letter in the word *diet* to see what you're allowed to eat. My favorite days were pie-it and fry-it.

My husband held his hand over his eye and groaned. Perhaps this time I needed to invent something a little more serious.

"Okay, kids," I said at breakfast. "Today your mom is going on a diet. I don't want to eat anything that will make me fat, and I need your help."

"Awww," said my son. "So no more brownies for breakfast?"

My husband glared at me.

"What?" I held up my hands. "I only did that once. I was tired."

"I know how we can help," said my daughter. "Tonight you won't even have to make dinner, so you won't be tempted! We can eat those two packages of marshmallows in the cupboard, and you can make yourself some dry toast." She beamed a benevolent smile in my direction.

"No, no, no!" I said, "I've invented something much more fun! It's called the 'hide and seek' diet. You guys hide all the goodies from me, and I won't be able to find them."

"Yaaaay!" shouted the children, and they rushed off to hide the goods.

It would've worked too, if it wasn't for the encouraging note I found on the fridge at lunchtime whilst nibbling on my piece of dry toast: *Mom, don't look behind my bed. There's nothing there. Love, your son.*

I headed straight for my son's bed. I wonder what . . . Oh, yes! The chocolate chip cookies left over from last night's game night!

I looked around furtively. I really shouldn't. But then again, America is a free country, and I invented this diet. I could do whatever I wanted.

Sweet freedom. I felt a swell of national pride as I crunched on my cookie. Or was it just a bigger swell over the top of my pants? In any case, in honor of my sudden devotion to my country, I decided to change my diet's name to "The American Diet," the diet where freedom reigns.

I pledge allegiance to the cookie, united with chocolate chips and milk. And to the hot dogs sold in stands, one cheeseburger, under ketchup, indivisible, with french fries and soda pop for all.

8

The Grandparent Visit

GRANDPA'S COMING! GRANDMA'S COMING!" YELLED MY CHILDREN, RUNNING around in circles as though someone were whipping them into a froth with a giant whisk.

Each week, my husband's courageous parents marched up to the door, bravely facing the wild and zany circus that was our family. I had to admire their courage. It seemed to me these people were the bravest of the brave. In the past, they had done everything from sticking their heads, or fingers rather, in a lion's mouth ("Wanna wiggle my loose tooth? Oh, sorry, I didn't mean to bite you. Are you bleeding?") to dealing with untrained animals ("Sorry about your pants, Grandma. Moo just started potty training last week.").

And finally, they've willingly engaged in death-defying acrobatics ("Thanks for showing me how you can do a headstand, Grandpa. That was really neat. Hey, do you need a wheelchair or something? You're walking kind of funny. Are you sure you're going to make it to the car?").

And still they kept returning. But this week, it was going to be different. Earlier in the day, I had given the kids a quick pep talk. "Kids, if any of you hurt, maim, or wet on your grandparents in any way, shape, or form, there is going to be big trouble!"

"How big?" asked my son, weighing his options.

I glared. "REALLY big!"

The kids all blinked in unspoken understanding.

And so it was with confidence that I swung open the door to welcome them in. "Mom! Dad! How nice of you to come!"

"Did you bring us any ice cream?" asked Hazel. "Our OTHER grandparents bring us ice cream every time."

"Ha-ha! Such a little joker she is," I said, nudging her hard toward the couch. "Let's all gather around the living room, children."

The children surrounded my parents-in-law and led them to the couch all shouting things at once.

"Hey, I can do a cartwheel!"

"See my new underwear? It's got spiders on it."

"Eeeew, I hate spiders!" shrieked Birdie.

"Wanna have a staring contest? Betcha you'll blink first."

My father-in-law held up his hands. "Kids, kids! If you don't quiet down, you'll never get to see what we brought."

"Is it ice cream?" yelled Hazel.

Grandpa laughed. "No, it's not ice cream. It's better than ice cream. It's a magic trick."

"Ooh . . . ," said the children.

Grandpa began to show them the magic trick between interruptions. "Does anyone . . ."

My daughter did a cartwheel in front of him.

"know"

My son climbed up on his lap to show him a picture.

My father-in-law looked at me. "Ahem. Is he?"

I nodded. "Yep. We finished potty-training him last month."

Grandpa smiled, relieved. "Well, now what's this a picture of, son?"

Moo said, "It's a picture of me dying. See? I have blood all over my face."

I choked. "He's going through a fear-of-death phase right now . . ."

Suddenly everyone quieted down as Grandpa lit a match.

"Okay, kids, wanna see a piece of paper defy gravity?" He took out a piece of translucent paper and held a match to it.

"Um," I said.

The paper began to burn and float up into the air.

"Um," I said.

Grandpa laughed. "Don't worry! It's going to disappear. Look, it's turning black. Here, I'll light another one."

"Can I try?" asked Birdie, taking the match in her hand.

"Sure!" said Grandpa.

"Um," I said.

"It looks like a giant black spider," said Scoot, watching it fall to the ground.

"Spider?" shrieked Birdie, dropping the match on Grandpa's pants, starting them on fire.

"Water!" I yelled. "Someone get some water!"

"No way!" Scoot shook his head. "You said we couldn't get them wet."

"Oh, man, not again!" said Grandma, staring at a growing wet spot underneath Moo, who was now sitting on her lap.

"I don't wanna die," sniffled the boy, sliding of her knees and running to me.

"Don't worry!" shouted Grandpa, slapping his leg with his hat in order to smother the fire. He backed toward the door. "It's just a flesh wound. Nothing a skin graft and a giant bandage won't take care of." He put on the blackened hat that he had used to smother the fire and limped a hasty retreat with Grandma close behind him.

"Wow," said Scoot, watching them drive away. "That must be a record. We hurt, maimed, and got them wet all in one visit. I wonder if they'll ever come back."

Of course they will, I thought. *They're grandparents—the bravest of the brave.*

9

Harry Potter Marriage Tips

ONE OF THE THINGS THEY TEACH YOU IN A MARRIAGE CLASS IS THAT communication is *the* single most important practice in a strong relationship. When the communication breaks down, so does the marriage. I take this counsel very seriously, which is why I read Harry Potter. This brilliant book by J. K. Rowling not only shows you how to turn your five yelling children temporarily into rabbits so that you can discuss important issues with your husband at family dinner (and now your children eat their vegetables), but certain characters in the book, such as the divination teacher, teach classes on communication skills such as clairvoyance and mind reading. These skills are vital in my marriage because my husband and I haven't been able to finish a sentence in thirteen years.

Me: "Honey, did you hear about the . . . Hey, son, don't try to stuff your mashed potatoes in your sister's shoe. You still have to eat them."

Husband: "Did I hear about wha . . ."

Daughter: "Daddy, Daddy, Daddy, Daddy, Daddy, Daddy, Daddy, Daddy, Daddy, Daddy, Daddy, Daddy . . ."

Husband: "What?"

Daughter: "Nothing. I just like saying your name."

Like I said, communication is the key to strong family relationships. This is why when you have children, you must learn to read minds or foretell the future so you can avoid disasters such as this:

Me: "Bacon! Last night I said pick up some *bacon* at the store on your way home!"

My husband (shrugging): "All I heard was pick up the b— before the baby fell into the soup, so naturally I assumed you meant that big screen TV we had been talking about."

As you can see from the above, almost true example, good communication is vital in a marriage. However, communication with your *children* is doubly important. Otherwise you could end up in a situation such as this: "When I said, 'dress your baby brother for the night,' I didn't mean dress him up as a knight!"

So, in order to save marriages and strengthen families everywhere, I have compiled a list of ten principles of divination that can help improve communication within families and increase effectiveness in any household.

- *Master palmistry.* Having your children show you their palms is extremely handy when trying to uncover the truth after they refuse to communicate what happened to your secret stash of Easter candy.

- *Focus your inner eye.* The Divination professor says you must never cloud your inner eye. If you can find one, it would surely be useful in discovering the hidden ketchup stain that your son spread all over the backside of your best silk shirt when he gave you a hug. (Unfortunately, the only way to get rid of the stain is through the complicated process of disapparating your shirt to a specialized dry cleaner most inconveniently located in Tibet.)

- *Wear huge, thick glasses and blink at people through them.* This is useful if you want to frighten your children's neighborhood friends away from your prize strawberry patch. (It's called "wordless communication.")

- *Sense an aura.* But don't try too hard, or you might sense that your teenager and her best friends just took their shoes off and stuck their smelly feet all over your brand-new couch.

- *Decorate yourself with lots of jewelry and big bangles.* This is extremely important in order for you to foster communication within your family. Don't ask me why—it just is.

- *Speak in a dreamy, misty voice.* This will be especially easy after the baby has kept you up all night. It is useful in avoiding conversations with the teacher about your son's behavior in school.

- *Sense clairvoyant vibrations.* This is an especially important skill to have when your husband takes out the sledgehammer and decides to remodel the bathroom for the third time in two years.

- *See past the mundane.* This is the hardest of all divination skills. Though difficult to master, this is one of your best tools. Some people, like me, are simply born with it. That is why the unidentified sticky stuff on the bottom shelf in my refrigerator has not bothered me in two years. It also helps with anger management too. Just see past that prominent place in the carpet where your son spilled a whole bottle of bleach last year.

- *Predict someone's doom.* I use this technique daily in order to make myself feel better after I have put my kids back to bed for the eighteenth time.

- *See symbols in tea leaves.* If you had noticed that X symbol in your peppermint tea, perhaps you could have predicted that your son was going to get his tongue stuck to the swing set during recess the other day, and you could have kept him home.

The techniques in the above list will definitely help you, and mothers everywhere, to at least think that you are improving your marriage and family through mind reading and clairvoyant techniques. And who knows? Perhaps your brightened aura will allow your husband to sense that you want a cruise to the Bahamas for your birthday present next year. Now *that* would really improve your marriage!

10

The Piano Preacher

A MOTHER IS REQUIRED TO PERFORM MANY HARROWING DUTIES DURING THE course of her day, including such nerve wracking roles as broken toe setter, expert tooth extractionist, goldfish funeral director, rancid shoe finder, and squirrel midwife. But the most demanding, rigorous, and bone-chilling role I have ever taken on in the course of motherhood is Piano Practice Drill Sergeant. It's a miserable job, requiring you to slog through the fierce jungle of your child's bedroom, searching for your next victim. Then, after bribing a younger sibling informant with a fistful of candy, you ferret a squealing child out of his or her foxhole, and drag the child, kicking and screaming to the piano. You often have to tie the child down to the piano bench with jump ropes until he or she pounds out "Go Tell Aunt Rhody" at least 176 times. Of course, you can't hear any of the notes because the child is complaining and yowling like a tortured cat the entire time.

I complained about this to my friend April. April is an expert mother who never sees the bad in anyone or anything. That is why I chose her to be my friend. She is completely blind when it comes to reality, so she can't see any of my faults and always says what I want to hear. You may argue that this characteristic would not make her the best person to come to for sage wisdom, but April has one important quality that makes her the perfect candidate to give me advice. She's usually the only one home whenever I have the dire need to complain.

"I can't stand it!" I wailed into the phone. "Piano practice is turning our home into a war zone. It's killing us!"

"That's because your kids don't have the right teacher," soothed April. "A child's best teacher is his or her mother. You have musical talent, don't you?"

"Well," I mumbled to myself, "my grandpa once taught me to play two chords on the harmonica." Then I grinned. "And I do play a mean set of spoons on campouts."

"See?" said April. "*You* should teach your children piano. Music in the home should bring joy and peace. You can teach your children the *joy* of music rather than the drudgery."

Now I may have my head in the clouds most of the time, but suddenly I had an attack of practicality.

"But . . . I . . . don't . . . know . . . how to play the piano . . . ," I said.

"Not a problem," April interrupted. "Piano teachers act like they know what they're doing, but have you ever noticed how much money they make you spend on books? It's because they cheat! They get everything they teach out of piano books. You know how to read a book, don't you?"

I thought back over my life experience. I guess I had taught lessons once before. As a young girl, I had taught my dog to twirl like a ballerina on his hind legs for a dog biscuit. Come to think of it, his little doggie lips did seem to curl back over his teeth as he danced. I think he was smiling! Maybe I did have some talent for teaching after all. If I could teach a dog to love ballet, I could certainly teach my children the joy of music.

The next week, I canceled piano lessons.

"But, Mom, we don't want to take piano lessons from you. It's bad enough when you harass us about our practicing," whined Violet, folding her arms in protest.

"Cheer up!" I said, giving her stiff, sulking body a hug. "There will be no more harassment in this family. Music is supposed to give you joy. It is supposed to be uplifting. That is our new motto! Only joy in music from now on. No more drudgery."

"Yay!" shouted the children.

I sat down at the piano with my first student.

"Okay," I said to my son, squinting sideways and trying to read the words without appearing to cheat. "First of all, let me hear your snails."

"Huh?" said my son.

I squinted harder at the page. "Uh, never mind. Why don't you just show me what you've been working on with your piano teacher."

He turned the page and started to pound out, "In a Wild Wigwam." It sounded pretty wild to me, sort of like a dog yipping when a little boy pulls its tail. For all I knew, that's the way it was written. What counted was that pounding on the keys as hard as he could and torturing the piano was giving my son some serious joy. Then halfway through, he stopped and pointed to a tiny letter beneath the notes.

"What's that?" he asked.

I squinted. "It's the letter *p*."

He rolled his eyes. "I *know* that. What does it mean?"

"Uh . . . It means 'perturbed.'"

"Perturbed?"

I nodded, and then, in a fit of pure genius, I added some practice incentive. "You're supposed to play it so many times that it perturbs your little sister and drives her nuts."

"Cool!" he said, starting to pound out the notes with more vigor than ever before.

I smiled to myself and hummed along. I had to admit, I was good. This was Joy-o-rama!

Violet stomped into the room. "Mom!" she yelled, covering her ears. "Tell him to stop! I can't stand it!"

My son grinned and pounded harder and faster.

"Ugh!" screamed Violet. "He's doing that on purpose."

"Ugh!" copied Hazel, sensing a way to needle her sister and moving in for the kill. "He's doing that on purpose."

"Mom!" yelled Violet.

"Mom!" yelled Hazel.

"Kids," I said. "Just look at how music is increasing the interaction in our home. Close your eyes and feel the music. Isn't it joyful?"

Pound, pound, pound, pound.

"Joy? You call this joy? Look at what she did to my arm," said my teen, showing me an angry red welt.

"She hit me first," said Hazel.

I smiled. "Love pats. Just look at that. I knew it would work!"

"Ugh!" screamed Violet, stomping her foot.

Pound, pound, pound, pound. My son was grinning maniacally.

The baby started to wail. At least I think he did. It was hard to hear over the shouting match and the joyful music.

Suddenly my husband walked in the front door and stopped in his tracks, looking stunned. "What is going on here?" he yelled over the cacophony of sound.

I ran over to give him a hug. "It's music, honey. Look what it's done to our home. Can't you just feel the love?"

He picked up the wailing baby before his older sisters could trample him while they chased each other, screaming insults.

"Love," he said. "Right."

"What?" I yelled.

"I said, 'I don't know how much of this love our house can take,'" he said, saving a toppling lamp with his left hand.

"But just look at our son," I replied. "He's so happy."

Pound, pound, pound, pound. Our son gave an evil laugh.

My husband looked at me. I cleared my throat. Maybe there was such a thing as too much joy in music. I guess those piano teachers really did know what they were doing. They were boring on purpose. Too much joy in music could be hazardous to your health. I decided then and there that I would beg our piano teacher to take us back the next week. *Whew.* The joy of piano. That's one job better left to the professionals.

11

Never Sniff a Gift Chair

I'M A PRETTY DOWN-TO-EARTH WOMAN. I'VE NEVER ONCE DESIRED LAVISH TRIPS to England, Scotland, or Indiana. I don't buy expensive perfumes, jewelry, or two-percent milk. No. My needs are simple. The only thing I ask is that my home be comfortable and welcoming . . . something like Windsor Castle perhaps.

Unfortunately, I have no money to make my home resemble Windsor Castle. But that doesn't seem to stop snooty decorating people, like my friend Nancy.

I like to hang around snooty decorating people like Nancy because they make me feel *really* down to earth, in a worm-eating-dust sort of way. But this is great. Because then I get to be snooty about the fact that *I'm* not snooty. It's that sort of a give-and-take relationship.

The thing I really admire about Nancy is the way she can sniff. The other day I was eating lunch at her house, and I noticed that she had changed her grandmother's antique coffee table from a lovely shade of olive-green, to a nice soft shade of gray. Of course, it looked fabulous.

"How do you do it?" I asked, looking up from my crustless cucumber sandwich. "Every time I come here you've done something amazing with your house. I love that color on your table."

Nancy smiled and sniffed delicately. "It's called, 'eggshell.' It's the newest trend in paint color: soft, soothing shades borrowed straight out of nature. I found the paint at a flea market, and it only cost me ten cents. You don't have to spend money when you decorate. You just have to remember the three Rs: repaint, refurbish, and recycle. "

Not a bad idea, I thought the next morning, as I tilted my head sideways and inspected my husband's favorite living room chair. "Don't you ever wish we had nice furniture?" I asked him as he headed out the door to go to work.

My husband squinted at the hairy, mustard-colored chair we had kept since our college days. "We don't have any money for new furniture," he said.

I tapped my chin with my finger and thought about the three Rs.

"Wait a minute!" My body tensed. "I've got it. I know just the thing! Grandma's gray-green sheet set that she gave us for our wedding. I'll reupholster the chair with the sheets." I ran down the hallway toward the bedroom.

"But I thought you hated those sheets," called my husband as I dug them out from under my bed. "You said they were the color of bird droppings."

"Yeah!" I replied. "Isn't that great? It's the newest craze. Colors borrowed straight out of nature. We'll actually be trendy. I'll be able to sniff at all my friends."

"Why would you want to sniff people?" he asked. "Don't you think that's a little weird? Besides, how are you going to reupholster a chair when you don't know how to sew?"

"Who has time for sewing?" I replied, heading for the staple gun in the garage. "I've got to get this done so I can invite Nancy over for lunch."

Two hours later, Nancy rang my doorbell. "Come in," I called, over the noise. *BAM, BAM*. I put a few last staples into the chair. *BAM, BAM, BAM*.

"It was so nice of you to invite me . . . What happened to your chair?" said Nancy, as she breezed into my living room. She had stopped breezing and was looking stunned.

I stood up and looked at the chair. "It's no longer hairy," I said.

"It's also no longer chair-shaped," she replied.

I cleared my throat. "It's called, 'Craters of the Moon.' It's the newest trend: lumpy shapes borrowed straight out of nature." I smiled and sniffed delicately. Then I coughed. Something was burning on the stove.

Nancy followed me into the kitchen. "Is that what we're having for lunch?" She pointed at the blackened noodles that slithered out of the saucepan into a serving dish.

I stared at it. "Don't you recognize it?" I replied. "It's French. I call it 'ramen brûlée.'"

Darn. I couldn't sniff at her because of all the smoke.

Ah, well. At least I didn't spend any money on the chair or the lunch. *But more important than that*, I thought as I looked over at Nancy politely choking down her noodles. *I'll never, ever have to worry about being snooty.* Sniff.

12

Roller-Mania

EVERYBODY HAS TALENTS. TAKE MY COUSIN BEANO, FOR EXAMPLE. WE CALL HIM Beano because his favorite pastime when he was a kid was flicking dried pinto beans at the back of people's heads. He never left home without them. Beano's main talent, however, is that he can convince you to do just about anything—especially things that, if you were in your right mind, might actually maim or kill you. Those are his specialties. This is why I found myself strapping roller hockey blades to my feet one fine Saturday afternoon at a local recreation center.

"Your mom was a regular roller queen back in the day. You should've seen her," said Beano to my children, who had all gone slack-jawed while waiting for me to figure out how to work the fasteners.

"Roller queen? Like roller skates? That's dorky, Mom," observed my son.

"Thanks," I said, standing up and wobbling around on my skates like a newborn colt.

"She never could figure out how to skate backward though, and one time when Davy Wilson asked her to couple-skate, she was making such enormous figure eights with her foot, trying to push herself backward that she swiped his feet right out from underneath him. It caused a pileup six feet high, along with two missing teeth and a broken spleen. After that, she was put on 'backward-skate probation.'"

"You *couple-skated*? That's disgusting," said Violet. "Can I move in with my best friend Gina? Her parents are normal."

"Hey," I said, starting to protest my dorkiness, when I noticed my children weren't listening to me anymore because I had wobbled too close to a handicap ramp. *This will end badly*, I thought, as I picked up speed, but luckily Beano caught the edge of my shirt with his hockey stick, and I ended up sprawled on my back before I could bowl over any innocent pedestrians.

"Maybe we should put her on 'forward-skate probation' too," said my son.

Violet helped me up and dusted me off. "Don't worry, Mom. I'll teach you how to skate."

"I'm telling you, she's a little out of shape, but she can do it," said Beano, snapping his gum and waving everyone toward the rink. "This lady was a great roller skater back in her day."

"What do you mean, 'a little out of shape'?" I called after him, trying to wobble and catch up to my three oldest children.

Violet took pity on me and helped me into the rink. "You're breathing kinda hard, Mom. Are you sure you're going to be okay?"

I shrugged off her hands, "Of course I'll be okay! I'm not old and decrepit, you know. I'm only thirty-eight years old for crying out loud . . ."

"Thirty-nine," replied my daughter. "You're almost forty. What if you break your hip or something? I heard that old people break their hips a lot."

I rolled my eyes as she steadied me in the middle of the rink. "I'm going to be fine. I'm sure I'll remember how to skate as I go along."

My daughter raised her eyebrows. "I don't know, Mom. That was an awfully long time ago." She handed me a hockey stick before skating away gracefully.

"Let's go!" cried Beano, tossing the puck on the floor, and all of a sudden I was standing still amid a blur of color whizzing all around me.

"Come on, Mom. Why aren't you moving?" yelled one of the blurs that sounded like my son.

"I don't actually know how to play hockey. What are the rules again?" I shouted into the fray. Suddenly I saw the puck moving toward me surrounded by several blurs.

"Okay. I can do this," I tried to convince myself. I attempted to skate backward in order to defend the goalie. Yes! I was moving. I was going backward!

"One question," I shouted, as the blurs closed in on me. I was headed straight for the goalie. "How do you stop?"

I didn't hear the answer because in the next second I had taken out the goalie and gone flying over the top of his sprawled body, crashing into the net.

"That's one way to stop," observed Beano. He snapped his gum and looked down at me. "Come to think of it, they never did take you off backward-skate probation, did they? Maybe that's a good thing."

I nodded. "I think I'll just go over to the sidelines and check my hips for injuries."

"Good idea, Mom," said my children.

Well, I thought. *It looks like Beano inherited most of the athletic talent in the family.*

I sat on the bench and looked around at the passersby with my hands resting in my chin. Suddenly I sat up and smiled. *Maybe I can develop a new talent*, I thought as I headed for our pile of jackets. *I wonder if Beano has any pinto beans in his pockets.*

13

Company's Comin'!

THERE'S AN OLD ADAGE THAT SAYS, "GIVE YOUR STRESS WINGS, AND LET IT fly away." I loved that quote until I realized that when I gave my stress wings, it turned into a giant mosquito. It kept coming back for more lunch and having lots of babies. Such was the case the other day when my husband called me an hour before dinner.

"Honey! Great news! I invited my basketball buddy Larry and his girlfriend over for dinner tonight, and they said yes! Can you believe it?"

I choked on the chocolate cake that I was feasting upon.

"Do you think you could have dinner and the house ready by six? I noticed the living room was in a bit of a disarray when I left this morning," said my husband.

"No problem," I said, clearing my throat and looking around at the problem. While I had been giving my stress wings with chocolate and a really great mystery novel, the children had gotten hold of a gigantic package of Styrofoam cups and used them as confetti. Now they were lying in the mounds of the white fluff and making "snow angels."

I briefly considered fleeing the country.

"Children," I said sweetly, clapping my hands together. "We've got company coming for dinner! Let's work together to clean up this mess."

"Yaaaaaay!" shouted the kids, jumping up and down and stomping all of the Styrofoam into little bits.

I rallied the troops and assigned out jobs.

"Why do I always have to clean the bathrooms?" whined Scoot.

"Because you're so good at it," I said. It wasn't exactly a lie; it was creative positive reinforcement.

He brightened. "Does that mean if I'm not good at it, you won't make me do it?"

I looked at my watch. "No, but I'll take you out to ice cream later if you can make it look like you cleaned it. Take Moo with you—he can help. He loves to swish things around in the toilet."

Forty-five minutes and several bribes later, you would never know the house had been planet Hoth.

Now, to make it look like I had slaved over dinner. I stomped around the kitchen, looking for something, anything, that I might be able to disguise as homemade. Aha! I lifted up a bag of tortillas. I could stuff these with the leftover Chinese takeout and call them egg rolls. They'd never know the difference.

The doorbell rang.

"Superman!" yelled my toddler as he shot past me with his blanket tied around his shoulders and a pair of underwear on his head.

"How many times do I have to tell you the baby is not a toy? Get those briefs off his head!" I yelled.

Birdie pouted. "But that's his superhero mask. See? He's even got eye holes."

I gave everyone within range an evil, "you better behave" stare, and then pasted a smile on my face. Then I swung the door open wide, "Lenny!" I cried. "It was so nice of you to come."

"That's Larry," hissed my husband out of the corner of his mouth.

"Nice Tweety-Bird slippers," said Larry as he walked in the door.

I looked down at my enormous fuzzy yellow feet. Darn. I was sure I had thought of everything. "It's sort of a Zen thing," I replied, serenely. "They remind me to let my stress fly away. Speaking of Zen and the orient—would you care for some homemade egg rolls?"

14

Mrs. Claus

ON THE FIRST DAY OF CHRISTMAS MY TRUE LOVE GOT FROM ME . . . A BOX OF cereal that I picked up for free. (Hey, I had a coupon, I might as well use it, right?) I couldn't help it. Last Christmas I suddenly felt like all our money was being sucked out of our pockets by giant invisible vacuums that lined the exits of all the stores in the mall. Thus, in self-defense, I turned into the world's cheapest Santa Claus. (So much so, my husband started calling me St. Nickel.)

"Honey, we need to go Christmas shopping tomorrow. It's getting a little late. What are we going to give the kids?" asked my husband the night before Christmas Eve, as I was cleaning up the supper dishes.

I laughed. "No worries. I've got all kinds of things in the closet. I shopped the after-Christmas sales last year and picked up all the toys that no one else wanted."

My husband blinked and stared. "Did you ever think there might be a reason that nobody wanted those toys?" he asked. "Besides, what are we going to get for our oldest? She's growing out of the toy stage. You know, I was thinking—"

I held up my hand. "I'm telling you it's all been taken care of. I found this great set of speakers on clearance for a dollar. She's going to love them!"

"One dollar?" My husband's voice rose. "What kind of speakers can you get for a dollar? And what are they for anyway?"

"Well," I huffed, "if you weren't so prejudiced against the Dollar Store, you would see that they have all kinds of neat stuff in there. I think they said they were for a car stereo or something."

My husband's eyes began to bulge. "Gee, hon, that's great. Considering she's only THIRTEEN, and she doesn't own a driver's license. Besides, how could they be on *clearance* at the Dollar Store if they cost a dollar?"

I looked up from my work in the sink. "Hey, you've got a point there. I think I might have been hoodwinked by some clever advertising."

My husband blew out a loud breath. Then I went back to my scrubbing. "Details, details." I waved a sudsy hand in the air. "Just trust me. It'll all work out." I put my last dish in the drainer and then dripped my way over to the garbage can.

"Yeah, but how?" asked my husband, trailing after me and handing me a towel. "What are you doing now?" he asked, watching me dry my hands and grab a bunch of newspapers.

"I'm recycling!" I grinned. "I'm going to spray-paint the handles of these tooth brushes that I put in the kid's stockings last year, and restuff them in their stockings for this year. They're going to love it!"

"Okay, that's it," said my husband, grabbing me by the elbow. "You're officially removed from any and all Santa duties this year. I'm taking over."

"What? You're firing me? You can't fire me! On what grounds?"

My husband yanked the toothbrushes out of my hand. "I'm dismissing you on the grounds of unlawful negligence of your Christmas duties and for cutting corners."

My mouth dropped open. "Cutting corners? Do you know how long I shopped the sales last January? I've got documentation." I looked around frantically until I spied my purse, which held receipts for the past ten years stuffed in every zippered pocket.

I pulled out a handful of receipts and waved them in his face. "You see? It'll never hold up in court."

My husband pulled a receipt out of my hand and began to read it out loud. "One cheeseburger, one item of fries . . ."

"Give me that!" I yanked the receipt back and stuffed it back in my purse. "Fine. I could use a little vacation." I stomped down the hallway. "And I'll be collecting all my unemployment benefits too," I called, "in the form of back massages and foot rubs."

That's when the coupon for free cereal fell out of my purse. I picked it up and smiled. At least I could still be Santa to one person in this house. Ha! Merry Christmas, true love! I wonder how I could hang a cereal box on a pear tree.

15

My Clown's Got Class

TEACHER CONFERENCES CAN BE THE MOST INFORMATIVE, EFFICIENT, AND effortless way to find out how your children are performing in the classroom. That is why I do my best to avoid them. When your child is the class clown, you don't exactly relish the opportunity to hear about his performances—especially when they involve homemade peashooters and the cute little blonde girl who sits in the front row.

In fact, I try so hard to avoid reports on my son's behavior, or lack thereof, that it's developed into a kind of strategic warlike game. I have turned to guerilla tactics to avoid being hounded by my son's teachers.

The other day when I noticed the school's number on caller ID, I used the old "hide in the jungle so they can't find you" guerilla tactic. I yelled, "Nobody answer that! It's probably a salesman trying to sell us vacuum cleaners."

The children showed their respect for their troop leader's every command by immediately jumping up and racing to answer the phone.

"Mommy, it's not a vacuum guy. It's the school."

Rats. How was I going to get out of this one? I looked over at my son. He had a bit of a tan. Maybe I could pretend to be from Mexico and speak only Spanish. I shook my head. The red hair and freckles were going to pose a bit of a problem with that scenario. Hmmm. Red hair. Too bad I didn't speak any Gaelic.

Suddenly my face lit up. Wait a minute! I was willing to bet the farm that the teacher didn't speak any Gaelic either! I picked up the phone.

"Holee?" (That was my knowledge of Spanish quickly converted into my not-ever-having-heard-a-single-word-of-Gaelic-in-my-entire-life guess at how they say "hello" in Ireland. Pretty clever, eh? I knew watching three thousand episodes of Sesame Street with my children would come in handy one of these days.)

"Mrs. Campbell?"

I decided to take it up a notch by inserting words vaguely recalled from my high school French class. "Comment allez uno dos?"

"Excuse me? Mrs. Campbell, are you trying to speak French or Spanish? I assure you, I am familiar with both languages."

Uh-oh. Man, this lady was good.

The next day I found myself slinking into my son's classroom wearing dark sunglasses and a large garden hat and holding on to the vain hope that I might be mistaken for the mother of the cute little blonde girl in the front row.

"Mrs. Campbell? Have a seat." The teacher pointed to a one-foot-tall chair in front of her desk. I scrunched into the pint-sized chair and looked up at her. This lady knew about guerilla tactics.

She frowned. "Mrs. Campbell, I wanted to discuss your son's behavior in the classroom. Here at Excellent Elementary, we pride ourselves in providing the best education in the state of Washington."

I smiled and nodded in agreement. Maybe she was about to tell me how my son was helping her to facilitate that education by offering to scrape gum off the bottom of the chairs during recess.

Her frown deepened. "But your son has a little trouble conforming to classroom expectations. Why, just yesterday the lunchroom monitors were complaining that he created a panic by starting a rumor that the cook blew her nose in the mashed potatoes."

They say you should be an advocate for your child during parent teacher conferences, so I smiled and pretended to dab my eyes with a tissue. "I always knew he was creative. Why, I remember—"

"Mrs. Campbell," she huffed, "*creative* doesn't begin to describe what happened yesterday during science. I was trying to teach the children to gently waft the scent of a chemical solution toward their nose so they wouldn't get overwhelmed. Your son decided it would be funny to take the whole bottle and put it directly under his nose and take a big whiff." The teacher paused, overcome by indignation.

"And?" I asked.

"And?" she repeated.

"Was it funny?"

Her eyes bulged. "Funny? Mrs. Campbell, I can see where your son gets his flagrant disrespect. Of course it wasn't funny! He almost fainted. I had to send him to the school nurse, who then complained that he tried to sell the leftover dessert from his school lunch to a child who was throwing up."

I tried to remain positive. "He's bold. He's entrepreneurial. He's—"

"He's a public nuisance!" the teacher cried. "What am I supposed to do with a child who tries to auction off the class mold experiments when I step out of the room?"

I sighed and shrunk down in my miniature chair. Well, at least I could take comfort in one thing. If no other career worked out, my son was going to make an excellent vacuum cleaner salesman.

16

Dance the Nylons Away

HAVE YOU EVER WISHED LIFE WAS LIKE A MUSICAL? PERHAPS YOU WOULD BE standing in the grocery store checkout line, waiting to buy a ham, when suddenly the cashier would burst into song about how ham was on sale for only $1.99 a pound. Then you would throw your ham into the air and dance while the bag boys lifted you on their shoulders and joined you in a rousing chorus. I haven't either.

That is why I found it so perplexing when the other day, as I was getting dressed, I heard a song on the radio that was so melodic, so hauntingly beautiful and moving that it made me want to toss my panty hose in the air and sing at the top of my lungs. And so I did the only thing I could think of. I leapt unto the bed and began to twirl and whirl and dance the expression of my soaring heart.

At first I was a little rusty. Not having danced ballet in, well . . . ever, it felt a little awkward. But then I started to warm up. I jumped. I pirouetted. I kicked and sang. Never had I felt such a surge of joy in my soul. *What was my mother thinking, not ever putting me in ballet?* I thought. *I could have been one of the greats! Why, just look at the way I can . . . ouch! Well, maybe not that, but what about this . . . and kick, and swoop, and . . .*

I heard a stampede of feet running. "Mom, what are you doing? You're bouncing on the bed with a pair of pantyhose," said my observant son.

"This is *not* bouncing. It's ballet. I'm expressing my jubilation!" I exclaimed. "I'm so joyful, I'm overcome."

"Seriously, Mom, you're going to hurt yourself," said Violet.

"No jumping on the bed!" yelled Moo.

Just then, the music on the radio built to a soaring climax. I decided to try something I had once seen an Olympic ice skater do on TV. I threw my arms up and leapt off the bed to attempt a triple toe loop in midair.

Unfortunately, in my exuberance, I flung the nylons up too high, and they became entangled in the whirling ceiling fan, knocking my leaping body off balance and slamming it into the corner of my mother's antique dresser. In an attempt to recover, I tripped backward over the pile of sheets and blankets at the foot of my bed and hit my head on the corner of the bookshelf. I slid to the floor and lay there for a moment, gazing up at the ceiling, where a tattered pair of black nylons circled over the heads of my brood of children, who had gathered around to stare down at my lifeless body.

My mother always said bad things happened to people who never made their beds. I should've listened to her.

From far away, I thought I heard a voice say, "Is she dead?"

Violet pointed her finger at me and said, "I hope not. Dead people start to stink after a while, and I've got a friend coming over later."

My son sniffed. "Well, something stinks around here. It smells like perfume . . . bleh!"

"That's just Oil of Youlay—that stuff old people put on their faces so they don't look so cranky," replied Birdie.

Then there was a giggle from the bed. Moo had begun jumping and spinning to the music on the radio. One by one, all of the children dove onto the king-sized bed and began to laugh and dance and twirl and fall over the top of one another.

"Stop . . . you're going to get hur . . . ," I croaked, trying to sit up. I stopped and watched in fascination as my spark of joy was ignited like a magical flame leaping from child to child. My heart swelled as I saw Hazel trip over her own two feet. We weren't the most graceful people on the earth, but I'd take this kind of performance over Radio City Music Hall any day.

17

Doctor, Doctor

ONE UNFORTUNATE SIDE EFFECT OF HAVING A BODY IS THE NEED TO GO TO THE doctor to get spare parts. Don't get me wrong—I believe in regular tune-ups, but the older I get the more humiliating it becomes.

I've had the same doctor for years: old Doc Slaughter. I trust him, even though he has a few quirks that are hard to live with. For instance, he likes to find stuff wrong with me. I don't like that. I've got enough self-esteem issues without finding out that I have an abscess on my innards. Call me crazy, but I like a doctor who'll tell me a balanced diet is a piece of cake in each hand. I don't want to know how many pounds I've gained since the last time I visited and how many dreaded diseases I've come this close to getting. I want death to take me by complete surprise. This is why every year I develop an ingenious plan to avoid Doc Slaughter's diabolical diagnoses.

This year, I walked into the doctor's office with my hair combed forward so that it covered most of my face. It was the perfect ploy! Besides distracting the doctor by forcing him to wonder about my sanity, it would ensure that he would not be able to diagnose anything from my neck up.

"Hey, watch where you're going, Chewbacca!" yelled the man whose wheelchair handle just stabbed me in the stomach. Admittedly, the risks might outweigh the benefits with this particular method of avoidance, so unless you've got great insurance, don't try it at home.

When the usual large, stern-faced nurse led me to the scale, I tried an old trick I learned from watching World War II movies with my dad.

"Step on the scale, please," directed the nurse in no-nonsense, nasal tones.

"I'm sorry. That information is classified. I cannot share it with anyone for national security reasons," I replied.

The nurse glared at me over her thick-rimmed glasses. Then she put her hands on her hips. "You're going to need *personal* security reasons if you don't step on that scale right now," she said.

Meekly I stepped on the scale.

"It doesn't help if you suck in your stomach," she said.

I let my shoulders slouch and my stomach puff back out to its usual shape. Man, why did I always get the Nurse Nazi?

"Hmmm." Her eyebrows rose cryptically.

"What?" I asked, annoyed. I hated it when she did that. Last year she had me thinking I was going to keel over dead the way she hemmed and hawed over my blood pressure.

"Been hitting the chocolate doughnut specials again, have we?" The nurse chuckled to herself as she seated me in the examination room.

"Ha, ha," I said.

Just then, old Doc Slaughter walked in. He was tall and gangly with a stork-like body that hunched over at the top. "What? Doughnuts, you say? I thought I told you to lay off those things. What was it that Hilde Bruch used to say?"

The nurse shrugged and continued to take my blood pressure.

"Oh yeah, oh yeah. I've got it," he said, clasping his hands together and staring down at me. "You can lead a person to cottage cheese, but you can't make him shrink!"

The doctor slapped his knee and wheezed and coughed until he could get his breath back.

"Funny," I said. Ever notice how skinny people love to tell fat jokes?

"Okay, okay. What seems to be the trouble?" he asked.

"Nothing," I said.

"Nothing? Then what are you here for?" he said, elbowing the nurse and exploding with another wheeze of laughter. Then he stopped. "Wait a minute, what—is—that?" he pointed toward my right eyebrow hidden behind a curtain of hair.

"I think I left one of my shoes back by the scale," I replied, sliding out of my chair toward the door.

He lifted my hair up. "Holy hamburgers, nurse, we've hit the jackpot!" He eyed the side of my head with glee. Then he tried to look serious as he asked me, "How long have you had that giant wart on your eyebrow?"

I yanked my hair back down over my face. "It's not a wart! It's a beauty mark." I stood up.

Doc Slaughter laughed. "Beauty mark, ha! That's a giant wart if I ever saw one. Hey, Spence!" he yelled through the open door. "Come and see the gigantic wart on this lady's eyebrow."

I squeezed my eyes shut when I heard the sound of running feet. Lots of them. Then Doc Slaughter said, "I could cut that thing off."

My eyes flew open. The doc had a bit of a maniacal gleam in his eye. They didn't call him Doc Slaughter for nothing.

"Maybe next time," I said, leaping up and trying to elbow my way through the crowd forming at the door. "I don't think my insurance would cover it—"

"Just tell them it gets caught on things—like the doorway," he yelled, chasing me down the hall. "Tell them it obstructs your vision."

It was time to implement my second-best plan of avoidance: Run!

Next year I'll have to come up with something better, like planting false beauty marks all over my face so the Doc can't find the real one.

Whew! That was stressful. Stress is unhealthy. I better get rid of it before it sends me back to the doctor. Can anybody point me to the nearest doughnut shop?

18

Mother's Day Is Comin' to Town

"Ohhh, I better not pout. I better not cry.
I better not shout. I'm telling you why . . .
Mother's Day is coming . . . to—day!"

THAT WAS THE SONG THAT WAS RUNNING THROUGH MY HEAD AS I LAY IN BED waiting for my breakfast to be hand delivered complete with scribbled love notes and lopsided clay sculptures denoting what an angel mother I have always been.

Not that I would ever pout . . . or cry. For heaven's sake, I'm a grown woman. And shout, ha! I hardly know the meaning of the word. Especially since Mother's Day is toDAY! Gee, I wonder what everybody's going to get me. Not that I'm expecting anything, because, of course, a mother embodies the role of selfless sacrifice, and if there is anything that I have done in the last . . . well . . . day or so, it is to sacrifice myself. Why, just yesterday I let my husband give me a nice foot rub so that he could feel more useful. And I did let Violet finish off my cold french fries at that burger joint the other day. Not that I ever eat at burger joints, because what kind of mother would let her kids eat all of that grease and saturated fat? But I do wonder how everyone will show their appreciation for all of the times I have taught them to clean the bathrooms—almost never pouting, shouting, or crying.

I clasped my hands together and wiggled my toes with excitement. I guess I did tell my husband not to get me flowers because they just die, but of course he knows that means, "Get the biggest bunch of roses you can lay your hands on, honey!"

Not that I'm expecting anything of course.

This is why I was so surprised when my husband paraded into the bedroom behind a gaggle of honking children, blowing on their kazoos while he sang lustily:

> *"Happy Mother's Day to you,*
> *You live in a Zoo.*
> *Because you have five children*
> *You often catch the flu."*

My husband grinned. "It's true, isn't it? Besides, it was the best poem we could come up with at six in the morning."

"Happy Mother's Day, Mommy!" yelled the children as they brought me a breakfast tray. I stared down at a glass of lumpy orange juice with specks of black floating around in it.

"Oh," I said, lifting up the orange juice. "What's inside this delicious-looking concoction?"

"We call it, 'Breakfast in a Glass,'" said my son. "We had a cinnamon roll and some orange juice, and we thought to ourselves, *Why not put it in the blender and invent a more efficient way to eat?*"

"Why, indeed?" I replied, choking down a sip and trying not to think of plump, steaming cinnamon rolls.

"Not only that," said Violet, "we got you a present!"

I sat up straighter. "A present? Why, you shouldn't have. I didn't expect—"

"Yeah, this year we didn't forget because of all the reminder notes you left on the mirrors," interrupted my son. He pulled a crumpled yellow sticky note out of his pocket. "Only twenty-one more shopping days until Mother's Day . . ."

"Reminder notes? Did I? Ahem. Well, now, I . . ."

My husband laughed. "Bring out the present, guys."

I sat perfectly still, trying not to let my anticipation overcome me while I heard shouts in the hallway.

"I'm going to give it to her."

"No, me!"

"You're not tall enough to carry it."

"Am TOO!

"ARE NOT! DAAAAAAAAAAAD!"

My husband excused himself to see what the trouble was, while I waited. I could hardly stand it. Not tall enough to carry it? It must be something big. I wonder what it could be? Perhaps they saw my sticky note on the fridge that said, "Happy is the Mother Hubbard who has a Pro Mixer in her cupboard."

Some loud grunting awoke me out of my reverie. *What in the world?*

My husband and four of the children were lugging a large orange container into the bedroom with my youngest son riding inside of it. As they got closer, my eyes widened.

"I can't believe it," I cried.

"Don't cry, Mommy," said my five-year-old.

Violet rolled her eyes. "Don't worry, she always cries when she's happy. Last year, she cried at the dolphin show at SeaWorld."

"Well," I said, sniffing, "they had such moving music going on in the background—"

"Never mind that!" said Violet. "What do you think of this great trash can we bought you?"

I swallowed, trying not to think about professional mixers. "It's lovely. I definitely needed more places to put my trash."

"We got you the latest model and the latest color," she said. "You'll be the most fashionable trash can owner in town."

I stared at the fluorescent orange garbage bin. "Thank you! I just know it will go perfectly with . . . ah . . . with . . . the sun, glowing orange through our kitchen window in the evening."

My children all beamed at me.

Then my three-year-old son climbed out of the trash can and onto my lap. "I've got a pwesent for you, Mommy,"

He reached inside the pocket of his jeans and pulled out a wrinkled piece of toilet paper.

I smiled down at him and stroked his chubby cheek. "Why, thank you, honey. I've always wanted some toilet paper. Just yesterday, I was saying to myself, 'I really wish I could have a spare piece of toilet paper in my pocket for odd jobs.'"

"Open it!" he commanded in his little boy voice.

"Oh, I didn't realize," I stuttered as I opened up the folds to reveal a dead gray potato bug, stiff with rigor mortis.

"His name is George."

I blinked.

My son smiled up at me. "I've been feeding him bwead cwumbs and keeping him in my pocket, so he won't be lonely. I wanted you to have him so you won't miss me when I go to pweschool next year." He stroked my arm lovingly with his dimpled fingers.

Suddenly I felt overcome with emotion.

"Oh no," groaned Violet. "Even insects make her cry!"

"Three cheers for Mommy!" yelled my husband.

"Hip hip hooray!" shouted the children as they monkey-piled me and poor George, who I never could find after that.

This time, I really was crying for happiness and composing another lovely poem in my head: *great and vast is a mother's joy, who gets squashed bugs from her little boy.*

To me, there will never be a better Mother's Day present in the world.

19

Keeping Up with the Bankses

FOR THE MOST PART, I AM A GOOD NEIGHBOR, SEEKING PEACE AND HARMONY with all citizens, animals, trees, and giant muffins. (Man, I love those things.) But seriously, having good neighbors is one of the wonderful blessings in this life. Take my next-door neighbors the Bankses, for instance. Harold and Hilary are the most stalwart of citizens, and are the owners of well-mannered pets, a grandchild with no tooth decay, and very, very, straight rows of petunias. But the best thing about them is that they are fine sports. They are my family's favorite sport, in fact, giving us hours of morning and evening entertainment comprising some of our grandest memories.

"Hey, Sis, remember when you stepped in the Bankses' beauty bark and moved it an inch to the left? Boy, were they mad!"

"Yeah, but not as mad as when the baby escaped from the bathtub and streaked naked across their front lawn during their garden club dinner party!"

It's not that we mean to make life difficult for them. It just happens; the main reason being that in everything from raising children to gardening, they are Mars and we are Venus flytraps, they are Roquefort and we are Easy Cheese, they shop at Macy's and we shop at the Dollar Store because we're too tired to get dressed up for Walmart. Needless to say, the Bankses have taken us on as their neighborhood project and love to offer helpful friendly advice over the fence, so to speak.

"You know," said Hilary, one breezy blue summer morning when she saw me weeding the roses next to her fence, "it's really a shame. This could be such a glorious rose garden. You realize you've got bugs all over your 'Peace' rose over there?"

"Rose garden?" I said, astonished.

"Yes! Why just look at that David Austin variety. I have one myself, you know. Yours is covered with bugs and rust. You really shouldn't overhead water. It promotes fungus. I've got some stuff in my greenhouse that will take care of it. I'll let you borrow it."

I shook my head. "Oh, thanks, but I couldn't do that."

Hilary looked confused. "Couldn't do what?"

"Get rid of the bugs or the fungus."

Now she raised one of her plucked eyebrows. "What are you saying? You don't want to get rid of your fungus?"

I shook my head.

"But," she stuttered. "Why not?"

"It keeps my boys entertained. They love anything brown and slimy."

She shuddered. "What about the bugs? Surely you don't want aphids crawling all over your flower patch?"

"Why, didn't you know?" I asked, standing up and putting a hand to my aching back. "This is not a flower patch. This is our aphid patch. We grow aphids, not roses."

Hilary stared. Then she feigned laughter. "Oh, you really are too much sometimes! An aphid patch—you can't be serious. You really had me going there."

I shook my head and bent back down to tug on some Canadian thistle. "But . . . I . . . am . . . serious, . . . Hilary. Oof!" I fell over backward, "You know how some people grow butterfly gardens?"

Hilary nodded.

I shaded my eyes. "Well, we like ladybugs, so . . ."

"So," said Hilary.

I pulled off my dusty, sweaty gardening gloves. "What do ladybugs eat?"

"Aphids," Hilary squeaked, backing away slowly.

I stifled a smile. "Hey, kids," I yelled to my children, who were dutifully pulling weeds and begonias out of my shade garden. "We've got a pretty good crop of aphids going this year!"

"Hurray!" they cheered.

"Not to mention the fungus!" I added.

"AWESOME!" yelled the boys, who came running toward me like a herd of buffalo.

I turned around to grin at Hilary, but she had already fled back to her greenhouse.

"You know, it's really a shame," I said to my boys, who were having a joyful time flicking aphids off of my 'Peace' rose. "Some people really have no sense of humor."

Scoot looked up. "Is she mad at you again?"

Then he took my pruners and cut a bug-infested rose, holding it out to me. "Maybe we could bring her flowers."

I surveyed the black-spotted leaves and watched a bug crawl out of the blossom onto his hand. I shook my head, tousling his hair. "No. I'm afraid I was a little rough on her this morning. I don't think flowers are going to cut it. But no worries. This afternoon I'll bring her a giant muffin. That'll fix everything."

20

Basketball Blunders

EVEN THOUGH I DON'T KNOW A SLAM DUNK FROM A GRAND SLAM, EVERYONE ELSE in my family takes sports pretty seriously. At our house, March Madness is a national holiday. In fact, we are such devoted fans that my son begged us to name our baby after his most idolized college basketball team player. When we failed to come through, he protested, and started calling the baby Mohammed. This earned us some pretty funny looks in public places when people tried to match the name with our freckled, red-haired toddler.

It was because of my son's sports mania that we signed him up for BASKETBALL CAMP for his tenth birthday. I capitalize all the letters in this word because this wasn't just any basketball camp. This camp was going to be taught by the players on my son's favorite college team, the Cougars. My son was over the moon! He was finally going to get a chance to meet his beloved Mohammed. It was a boy's dream come true, and I wanted to be there to see it.

Unfortunately, my son did not want me to be there to see it.

"Mom, could you maybe stand, like, ten feet over that way?" he asked me as we were standing in line to enter the huge coliseum where the sacred event would take place.

"Ten feet which way?" I said, smoothing down a cowlick on the back of his head.

He shook my hand away. "Mom, please. Over there, behind that pine tree."

"Behind a tree? Why?" I licked my thumb.

"Mom!" he hissed. "Don't be putting spit on my head. Now please! Go over there!"

"Why do you want me to stand over there?" I asked, resisting an urge to smooth down his wrinkled T-shirt.

"Because," he whispered out of the corner of his mouth, "you're a mom."

"Of course I'm a mom." I laughed. "I'm *your* mom. I birthed you didn't I?"

"Shhhhhh!" he interrupted. His eyes shifted nervously to the boys standing in front of him. "I can't believe you just said *birthed* out loud." Then he leaned over and spoke in my ear. "Mom, you're killing me. Do you see any other moms around here?" He leaned back and folded his arms. His eyes were pleading.

I looked around. "Oh," I said sheepishly. "I get it. You don't want to seem uncool." I handed him his backpack, trying to dodge his hand pushing me away. "Okay. Okay. I'm going. I'll just be behind that little pine tree over there." I pointed at a wispy baby pine close by. "Don't worry. I'll be right here if you need me."

"The big pine tree, Mom—all the way behind it." My son pointed at an enormous pine tree in the opposite direction.

"Fine," I said, backing away, "the big pine tree. Don't worry. I'll be all but invisible." I covered my eyes to indicate invisibility.

"Promise?" said my son.

I nodded, giving him a thumbs-up and continuing backward down the hill toward the hundred-foot-high pine tree. Each time he looked at me, I gave him the invisibility sign by covering my eyes in order to reassure him. Maybe that was a dumb idea. If I had been looking where I was going, perhaps I wouldn't have stumbled into that gopher hole. One minute I was walking backward with my eyes closed (well, okay, maybe normal people don't walk backward with their eyes closed) but then suddenly—*bam*! The ground opened up and swallowed my foot. With a yelp, I flew backward into the pine tree and sent the contents of my purse flying in all directions.

I looked over at my son. He had pulled the hood of his sweatshirt over his head and tightened the strings until only his nose was sticking out. Well, so much for invisibility. I gathered up the contents of my purse and tried to slide nonchalantly behind the pine tree amid the snickers of the boys. I glared. Whatever happened to male chivalry? Was there no respect for elders in this day and age?

It was while I was glaring at the boys that I noticed something. These boys were not the kind of ten-year-old boys I was used to. Instead of wrinkled T-shirts and ratty shoes, these boys had basketball *outfits*! They had shiny duffle bags and hundred-dollar basketball shoes. The boy ahead of my son was showing him an autographed leather basketball.

My heart sank. How was my son supposed to compete with that? I watched my son trying to look cool in his beat up Keds, and I bit my lip. Had I made a mistake sending him to this camp? Would he come home feeling like he didn't measure up?

I thought for a minute, and then suddenly I knew what to do. As they say in basketball, "The best defense is a good offense," so I quickly cooked up an ingenious offensive maneuver. Not only would I make my son happy by leaving, but I was going to build up his self-esteem before I disappeared!

I sidled out from behind the pine tree and yelled to my son, "I'm going to take off, now. See you later. Have a great time!" Keeping with my plan, I gave him a surreptitious "I love you" sign in sign language while I was talking. It was brilliant! No one but my son would notice the subtle sign of affection.

My son refused to look at me.

I tried again.

He looked at sky.

I tried to get his attention by waving my sign in the air.

"Bye now!" I blew him a couple of kisses when I thought he saw me out of the corner of his eye. He turned his back toward me. Man. This was going to be harder than I thought. How was I supposed to give him a subtle self-esteem boost when he was ignoring me?

"Hey!" I yelled, forgetting subtle. "Did you hear me?" My son turned toward me giving me an exasperated look. Undaunted, I threw him all my signs of encouragement. No son of mine was going to feel second rate. *Ha*! I thought, grinning at the other boys. *My son may not have basketball shoes and duffle bags, but he's got a mother who loves him*!

I was wildly blowing kisses and giving I love you signs when I saw my son's eyes widen in horror. I followed his line of vision and saw a dark-haired college boy in maroon basketball shorts staring at me like I was a lunatic. He thought I was blowing kisses and making "I love you" signs at him. He backed away and veered to the left in order to avoid me, and it took a moment before I realized that it was Mohammed, the most famous Cougar basketball player, and my son's idol. He was followed by the rest of the guys on the Cougar team. They were laughing and blowing him kisses.

I turned to look at my son. He was gone. I saw his ratty tennis shoes peeking out from underneath the hundred-foot pine tree.

Sheesh. Sometimes nothing a mother does turns out right. I slunk away to the car, hoping my son would speak to me again someday. I'd make it up to him somehow. Maybe with a brand-new pair of basketball shoes.

21

Now We're Cooking with Gas

ONE OF THE BEST TRADITIONS IN CUB SCOUTING IS THE BLUE AND GOLD banquet. This event was obviously invented by a mother. I know this because not only does the blue and gold banquet get women out of cooking dinner, but the conceivers of the celebration also thought up a way to redesignate who had to bring the potluck item by making up a thing called "The Cub Scout Cake Baking Contest."

"No adult must in any way, shape, or form help the Cub Scout make his cake," said the rules on the paper my son handed to me a couple of hours before the dinner. "No adult can even come up with the idea for the cake. There must be *no adult participation at all* when the cake is made."

"Ha!" I said to myself as I read. "Pure genius!"

Or so I thought . . . until my son actually tried to bake a cake all by himself.

"Mom," whined my son, "how am I supposed to make a cake? I've never made a cake before."

I mustered up a sympathetic look. "I know. I wish I could help, but it clearly says here under rule number three, 'No adult participation.' You wouldn't want me to be dishonest now, would you?"

My son shook his head, and I put down the rules and gleefully went back to mopping the floor and ignoring the fact that there was a cake to be made.

"Did I hear people say they were baking a cake?" asked Violet, skidding into the kitchen in her bare socks. "I know how to bake a cake. I can help."

"I don't know," I said, remembering the last time I left her alone in the kitchen, and she ended up using my good sewing scissors to cut up some chicken. I picked up the paper with the rules. "It says right here in rule number three . . ."

"I know, I know," said my daughter. "I heard you say 'no adult participation,' but I'm not an adult, I am a teen. So technically, I'm allowed to help, right, little buddy?" She reached over and tousled my son's wiry red hair, and then she put her arm around his shoulders and pulled him into a hug.

His body stiffened. "I'm not your little buddy," he said.

I frowned, staring at the rules. "Well, I guess they didn't say anything about siblings not helping."

"There, you see?" she said, taking my arm and steering me out of the kitchen. "Now you go rest your feet and let me do all the work."

Rest my feet? Do all the work? Now that was a new one. Maybe my sleep-in-until-noon teenage daughter had turned over a new leaf.

I decided to take her up on the offer.

"Don't make a mess," I called, nestling down into my favorite reading chair. "And don't waste anything," I said, tossing in a family value for good measure.

"Okay, Squinty," I heard my daughter say. "What kind of cake do you want?"

"Don't call me Squinty, or I'll tell your friends you have smelly feet," said my son. "And I hate cake, so why should I make one?"

My new and improved teacher/daughter/chef refused to be goaded. "You hate cake? That's just weird. What do you like then?"

"Oreos," he said.

"Hmmm," my daughter replied. "An Oreo cookie cake. I can do that."

"Really?" asked my son. "You've got a recipe?"

"Recipe?" she scoffed. "I don't need a recipe. Cooking is an art. Using a recipe is cheating."

"But Mom says—"

"Just go get a package of cookies out of the cupboard. Then watch me and learn," my daughter said in her most dramatic tone of voice.

For the next half hour I sat stiffly in my chair trying to ignore the bangs, crashes, and insults I heard flying across the kitchen.

"That doesn't look like a cake."

"What do you mean? This is the greatest cake ever. It's going to win first prize in the contest for gifted and exceptional creativity. I bet no one ever thought of assembling a cake in the shape of the human digestive system before," gloated my daughter.

"It certainly looks digested," said my son.

"You be quiet. It was all your fault the Eiffel Tower fell over and we had to improvise."

"My fault? How was it my fault? You were the one who tried to snitch a piece from the bottom, *and* you kept eating all the batter. That's the only reason you wanted to help me."

"I don't want to hear it," yelled my daughter. "Now get going on separating and crushing those Oreos, while I mix up the frosting."

I forced myself to sit in my chair throughout the whole process until I heard whispering and then a loud yell, "Watch where you aim that thing, will you? I don't want any of my body parts burned off."

No longer able to stand it, I leapt out of my chair and ran into the kitchen in time to see my daughter pull her father's welding mask down over her face and aim a blowtorch into my best mixing bowl.

"What in the world are you doing?" I screeched, yanking the blowtorch out of her hand.

"The frosting was a bit stiff," said a muffled voice from behind the mask. "I was going to soften it up a little."

"Okay, that's it," I said, tearing the bowl out of her hands. "I don't care what it says about no adult participation. I'm supervising the rest of this cake-making business."

I heard a groan coming from the table behind me. I whipped around to see my son slumped behind a mountain of separated Oreo cookies.

"Great job!" I said. "What did you do with the creamy parts?"

"Oooooooooh," he groaned, holding his stomach.

I turned to my daughter. "Did you tell him to eat all those middles?"

She shrugged. "You said not to waste anything."

"What have I done?" I said, covering my eyes with my hand. Then I looked at my watch and panicked. "Never mind the frosting. It's five o'clock. The banquet is starting! We're just going to have to take this cake naked to the banquet."

"Quick!" I yelled to my son over my shoulder, as I ran to gather up the rest of the family, "Hurrytothegarage, andcutoutcardboardinthesizeofthe-cakeandcoveritwithtinfoil! Run!"

When I returned to the kitchen, I found that my son had followed my instructions precisely. Under a foil-wrapped ball of cake was a little piece of cardboard.

I sighed as I scraped bits of foil-wrapped digestive system onto a plate. What insane person ever thought up the blue and gold banquet and its evil cake baking contest anyway? Obviously NOT a mother.

22

Dangerous Liaisons

THERE ARE SOME PEOPLE WHO IT IS JUST PLAIN DANGEROUS TO BE AROUND. TAKE my sister Darcy, for example. Of all the people I could choose to befriend in the world, she should be the last. We are just plain bad for each other, and crazy things happen when we're together. This is why I hang out with Darcy almost every day. I just can't resist the temptation to see what will happen next.

The problem is that because of some freak genetic mix-up in heaven, we both inherited exactly the same faults. This may not seem like a big deal, but actually, it is a highly volatile situation. When two people with the same faults start hanging around each other, the world better watch out, because eventually the faults see each other from across a crowded room, wink, and say, "Hey, let's get together." Soon they are married and having baby faults of their own. Before you know it, they are multiplying until both the fault owners have so many character flaws it is a wonder lightning doesn't strike them both dead in their tracks right then and there.

This was especially true for Darcy and I when we were both first-time mothers. As anyone can tell you, one of the qualities every first-time parent develops almost instantly is the ability to see everything their own child does as pure genius, and Darcy and I were no exceptions. In fact, we were worse than most people because our vanity would feed off of each other until it grew into something monstrous and completely out of control. Several times we almost came to blows.

"Would you look at that!" Darcy marveled as she elbowed me hard in the ribs and pointed to my newborn and her three-month-old, who were having a playdate on the floor of her living room.

"Ouch! Look at what?" I asked, rubbing the side of my rib cage.

"There! Right there! Look at what my precious little Egbert is doing."

I squinted at the babies. "It looks to me like he's rolled over. No, wait. He is sucking on the top of my daughter's head."

Darcy let out a dreamy sigh. "Isn't that amazing?"

I stood up. "Amazing? Your son certainly shows an early talent for giving head-hickeys," I said, snatching my daughter away from her immoral cousin. "What kind of a kid wants to suck on people's heads, anyway? I'd watch that boy if I were you. You never know where this kind of thing might lead. Why I had an uncle who—"

"No, no, no. It's not that," she said. "It's your daughter's red hair. Egbert must have such a fine appreciation for color, taste, and texture. He's already showing the signs of the famous chef he'll become someday. It's obvious to me now that he's a child prodigy. I don't know why I never saw it before. I'm such a bad mother."

"There, there." I patted her on the back. "You shouldn't feel bad. Why it was only just now when you mentioned your son's passion for beauty and texture that I noticed my daughter was letting him eat her scalp without complaint. I should have realized way before now that she has the patience of a saint. She's obviously meant for diplomacy. I'll be so proud to be the mother of the first woman president."

Things went on like this for a while until time and experience helped us to see just how naïve we had been. We finally realized that our children were not only gifted, but they were also clearly smarter than every other child their age.

"You know," I said to Darcy one day as I held up giant reading flash cards to the toddlers. "It's obvious to me that our children are not getting enough mental stimulation in the nursery at church. When I poked my head in the other day, they were coloring, of all things."

"Coloring!" said Darcy. "Why, our children mastered coloring at the age of nine months. You could just tell by the way they scribbled that they understood the finer intricacies of how color, line, and structure worked together to form an abstract work of art."

"And you should see the childish picture books they read to those children." I shook my head. "If they only knew our children could understand and read actual words."

I held up a giant flash card. "What does this say, Egbert?"

"DA!" he said, pointing to the tall red word that said *Daddy*.

"And how about this?" I said, holding up another one.

"DA!" he said.

Darcy clasped her hands together and beamed.

"See?" I said. "I wonder if we should discuss this with the nursery teachers."

Darcy shook her head, "I don't know. Our kids have only been in there for one week. Do you think they'll take us seriously?"

We stared at our gifted children, both of us lost in our own thoughts. Egbert was showing his predisposition for fine cuisine by chewing the corner of one of the enormous flash cards.

The next day, we invited one of the nursery leaders to my house for lunch.

"You want to what?" she asked, choking on her apple.

"We think our children's intellect is languishing in the younger nursery," I told her, my voice rising with excitement. "They know everything there is to know about coloring, and they're already thankful for fish and for flowers."

I gave a dramatic pause to let the teacher soak this in.

"That's why we were thinking they should skip a grade," Darcy finished for me.

I nodded, and the nursery teacher blinked at me.

"Two grades actually," added Darcy. "We're pretty sure they're ready to sit in with the five-year-olds."

The nursery teacher looked from me to Darcy and then back again. Then she laughed. "Ha! Oh, that's a good one. You really had me there!"

Then she realized we were serious. She stood up and began to gather her things. "Give me a week to talk to the other teachers," she said as she left.

I looked over at Darcy. "That went well," I said. "Of course, we didn't showcase all of their talents. Do you think we should have showed her how they can eat their spaghetti without using their hands?"

Two weeks later, Darcy and I were asked to be teachers in the nursery. I sat on the floor with the children, holding up an enormous flash card with giant red lettering on it that said "Fish."

"Da!" said the children, pointing at the card.

"No, no, no!" I cried, "It says fish, F-I-S-H, fish. We're thankful for fish. You know, like this." I blew pretend bubbles and waved my fins in the air.

The children stared at me. One little girl started to cry.

I looked up. The old nursery teachers stood watching me through the window in the door. They smiled and waved.

Darcy and I glared back. Oh well. At least we could control the mental stimulation that our gifted children received. *Now*, I thought as I searched through my things, *time for singing time. Where did I put the recording of my husband singing songs in the shower? It's never too early to start learning opera.*

23

Kids Really Come in Handy

ONE OF THE FIRST LESSONS YOU LEARN WHEN YOU BECOME A MOTHER IS THAT you can't do everything. Suddenly the tasks that face you every day are more than any one person can accomplish. That's when you learn to delegate—until you realize that three-year-olds can't clean bathrooms and neither can teenagers. So you learn other methods of coping, such as closing your eyes when you inspect the toilets and thinking of the unidentified stuck-on bits in your cereal bowl as a new category in the basic food pyramid. Using these and other lower-your-standard-type methods, you can feel pretty good about delegating just about anything to anybody.

This philosophy sometimes upsets my husband, however, who doesn't share my forward-thinking ways.

"Honey," he said to me in between bites of oatmeal one morning, "Why is Moo carrying around a hacksaw? We've got to supervise that boy. He gets into everything when we're not looking."

"A hacksaw?" I slapped my forehead. "I told him he needed a sledge-hammer. What was he thinking? Doesn't anyone around here ever listen to instructions?"

My husband choked. "*You* told him to get a sledgehammer? What, do you have a death wish for the all the furniture in our house? The hole in front door still hasn't been patched from when you gave him my old cordless screwdriver for Christmas!"

I shrugged. "What? He's a boy. He likes to work with tools."

My husband stared at me. "He's three. Why can't he play with rubber balls like other three-year-olds?"

I shook my head. "Rubber balls don't teach important skills like tools do."

My husband set down his spoon and rubbed his forehead. "Exactly what kind of skills can a child learn from a sledgehammer?"

Just then, Violet ran shrieking through the kitchen waving a fistful of papers in the air. "Mom! Tell your son it's not nice to chase people with dangerous weapons." She screamed once more before she disappeared through the sliding glass door behind my husband.

"Tell her to give me back those papers," yelled Scoot as he rounded the corner, wielding my husband's best hammer. "I'm not done reading them!"

I smiled. "See? Hammers teach negotiation skills. Very important."

My husband's chair scraped as he stood up suddenly and threw down his napkin. "Okay. That's it. What is going on around here?"

He whipped open the curtains to the sliding glass door that looked out over the backyard. "Wha . . . ?"

I walked over and proudly stood beside him. "Isn't it great? Just look at how industrious they are."

He stood there mutely watching our five children taking the new trampoline out of its box and flinging the parts all over the lawn. Violet stood on the platform of the swing set, yelling commands, while Scoot sat underneath a tree, wrinkling his forehead and squinting at the instructions for putting it together. My other two daughters were hooking the springs together into a long chain and trying to jump rope with them.

My husband looked at me.

I grinned. "What? You said you didn't have time to put it together this week, so I told the kids they could do it themselves. Aren't you glad you have such talented children?" I patted his back and pointed out the window. "I think they get their handiness from you. What do you think?"

My husband's face grew haggard when he heard Violet yell at her brother. "I told you we don't need the instructions! I took a stained glass class in school, for crying out loud. I know how to put this thing together already!"

He let the curtains drop and walked over to the edge of the table with his shoulders stooped. Silently, he picked up the sack lunch I had made him for work. Before he left, he looked back at me from the doorway and croaked, "Tell me when it's over, so I can come home." Then the door slammed shut behind him.

Later that night, I was stir-frying a chicken when I heard the front door creak open slowly. I wiped my hands on a towel and went to greet my husband.

Only his head was showing behind the partially open door. "Is it done?" he whispered. "Nobody maimed or killed?"

I laughed. "You're such a worrywart." I threw down the towel took his hand, yanking him back outside and tugging him toward the backyard.

"You came home just in time," I said. "The kids have been working so hard. They've been calling me outside to help them hook on the last spring."

He groaned as he followed me, but then he stopped and stood up straight, staring at what looked amazingly like a trampoline. The kids were straining to pull the edges of the canvas and holding the sides down so that our oldest son could get the last couple of springs on.

"Well, well," he said, striding over to help with the last one. "I always knew you had my talent for being a handyman," he said, ruffling the cowlick on the back of our son's head.

"Hey! What about me?" said Violet, rolling off the other side of the trampoline where she had been lounging. "I'm the one who told him how to put it together!"

Scoot let go of the canvas. "You did not. You just tried to act like you knew what you were doing. I was the one who read the instructions."

"I put on the legs!" yelled Hazel.

"Calm down," said my husband cheerfully, as he snapped the last spring in place. "It's all done! Now you can play."

"Hooray!" yelled the children as they all let go of the edges.

Suddenly, my husband's smile froze as a terrible creaking sound filled the air. We watched in horror as the whole trampoline slowly tipped onto its side and curled up into a giant taco around my husband's rigid body.

"Aaaaaaargh!" howled my husband in a strange voice that set the neighborhood dogs barking.

"I knew I should have put my foot down this morning," he said, clenching his hands around the springs and shaking the bars of his prison. "Now I'm going to have to take the whole trampoline apart and put it back together again." He squeezed his way out of the taco and sank down into a lawn chair, putting his head in his hands. The kids tipped the taco back up on its feet.

Suddenly I smiled. "You thought we were putting together a trampoline?" I said, employing my best "standard lowering" coping skills, well-honed from years of delegating. "That's no trampoline," I said, pointing at the children gleefully sliding down the steep sides of the taco. "That's a ski hill. You're never too young to start training for the Olympics!"

Sheesh! I thought the next day, as I watched my husband stomp around and complain about how long it was going to take him to fix the giant taco. *Some people really need to learn how to delegate!*

24

Treasure My Trash

THERE'S NOTHING I LOVE MORE THAN A YARD SALE. THE THRILL OF THE HUNT, the scent of a bargain, and the chance that I might strike it rich with that giant antique purple pig vase unearthed from beneath someone's moldy shoe collection gets me out there every weekend. The problem is, I just can't resist a deal—any deal, whether I need it or not: recipe books, exercise videos, bottles of drain cleaner, you name it. If it's cheap, I buy it. Who knows when another deal like that might come around? This is the reason for my old, broken-down dresser collection, also accumulated from years of shrewd yard sale hunting. The more drawers I have in the house, the more junk I can put in them. I know, I admit it. I have a problem.

Never was this more apparent than the weekend I came home with masses of kitchen utensils from the estate sale of someone down the street. I slammed the door of my car and ran up the sidewalk to the steps of my house, my arms weighed down with bagloads of jingling treasure. I couldn't wait to show my husband my pile of plunder.

"HALT! Who goes there?" said a voice. My progress was suddenly cut short when a miniature person wearing camouflage pants and my best metal strainer for a helmet barred the entrance to the house with a broomstick.

"Son?" I squinted at the face beneath the helmet, which had slid down over his eyes and rested precariously on his nose. "Is that you?"

Scoot pushed up his makeshift helmet and said, "Oh. Hi, Mom."

"Hi, Son. Good to see you. Is your dad home?" I tried to push my way past him, but the broomstick stayed put, blocking my advance.

"The general will see you in a moment," said my son.

"Okay, soldier," I said, smiling and lifting off his helmet, "let me through. I've got work to do inside the house."

My son frowned and snatched back his helmet. "Stand down, ma'am. I have my orders. No one is to come inside this house before going through an official inspection. We've got to be sure you're decontaminated and de-junkified."

"Decontaminated?" I took a step back. "What are you talking about?"

My son leaned over and whispered, "Daddy's de-junking the house. He says I can't let anybody in—especially any ladies fitting your description."

My mouth hung open. "Ladies fitting my description?" I said. "Okay. That's it. The joke's over. Let me in, or there's going to be some serious—"

He stood back up, his back ramrod straight. "I'm sorry. The general in charge says . . ."

"General in charge?" I yelled. "I'm the general in charge around here!"

"Not anymore," said a voice behind my miniature soldier. Violet emerged from the dim recesses of the living room beyond the doorway and continued, "We've had a military coup while you've been away."

My brows shot down. Military coup? What was this all about?

My son leaned toward me and whispered out of the corner of his mouth, "Watch out for this lady. She's the inspector. And she's mean as a snake." He jerked back to attention when my daughter shot a glare in his direction.

The inspector snapped her fingers, and two minions emerged from the shadows, holding trash bags.

"Yard sales!" I cried. "I was just at some yard sales down the street!" I looked at Hazel. "You. Go get your father."

"Belay that order," said Violet. Then she walked toward me with a menacing look and pointed at the load in my arms. "What do you have in those bags?"

I squeezed the bags to my chest, my eyes widening. "Nothing. Just some useful things for the kitchen. Hey! Give that back!"

I tried to snatch the wooden spoons and rotary beaters from the greedy little hands that tore the bags away and threw them on the sidewalk. They were giggling and stuffing my hoard into their trash bags.

Violet, turned watchdog, picked up a broken cheese slicer. "Useful?" she said. "You call this useful?" She tossed it to one of her underlings.

"Hey," I yelled. "You can fix that wire!"

"Junk!" she cried, picking up an old spice rack.

"No! It's not junk," I said, bending over. "Just look at how this meat mallet glistens in the sun. You could use it for a Christmas ornament if you wanted to."

The inspector straightened, unsmiling, and folded her arms. "Dad says not one more piece of junk can cross the perimeter of this dwelling without ten other pieces of junk leaving the premises. What are you going to give up in order to bring that meat mallet inside?"

Argh. I blew through my lips in frustration, watching them confiscate all my treasure. *Just when all my collections were starting to be interesting*, I thought. I wondered if these soldiers could be bribed if I greased their palms with some bubble gum from my purse.

Later that night, I sat on the couch in front of the television, watching an old rerun with my husband, the general.

"You know," he said. "You're taking this awfully well. I thought you would be more upset when I decided to organize all the closets and cupboards."

I smiled and patted his knee. "You know me," I said. "My even-tempered, carefree personality makes me pretty easy to live with."

He raised an eyebrow and stared, but he didn't pursue the subject.

I just smirked and fingered the hastily scribbled note with a child's handwriting that resided in my pants pocket. It was written by my soldier son. Apparently there was a black market for kitchen utensils under his bed. For the right price, anyone could smuggle an old meat mallet or two inside the house.

25

Please Don't Make Me See the Principle

ONE OF THE FIRST THINGS I LEARNED AS A MOTHER IS THE IMPORTANCE OF teaching correct principles. I remember rejoicing one day when I read one wise man's counsel to teach people the correct principles, and then let them govern themselves.

This is great news! I thought to myself as a parent. All this time, I had been trying to *govern* my children! What a fool I'd been. It was right there in black and white that if I taught them properly, they could govern themselves. With joy, I raced home from church in order to start experimenting.

"Okay, kids," I said to my children that night. We all stood gathered in my son's bedroom, staring down at his pillow. "This," I said, pointing, "is a bed."

My teenager, Violet, lifted up one eyebrow. "What do you mean? Of course it's a bed."

"Hush," I said, holding up my hand for silence. "I'm teaching you correct principles. You must listen so you know what to do."

Violet rolled her eyes and folded her arms.

"Now," I resumed my speech, "does anyone know what a bed is for?"

"Jumping on," shouted three-year-old Moo proudly. He had recently developed the unfortunate habit of unmaking all the beds in the house in order to use them as trampolines. He tried to scramble up on his brother's bed in order to demonstrate, but I held him back by his collar.

"Yeah," agreed Scoot, "and it makes an awesome barrier to hide behind when you're having marshmallow fights with your sister." He reached down and pulled a petrified marshmallow from under his pillow and popped it into his mouth.

My eyes narrowed. "You've been having food fights in here?"

"He-he," laughed Scoot.

I glared.

"What?" he protested. "You told us to make up games when we were bored and not to bother you."

I closed my eyes and slowly breathed through my nose. Boy, that yoga class I took when I was first married was really proving useful in times of stress. I never knew how much I was going to need it after I had kids.

"Could we get on with this?" said Violet. "I've got at least ten steps left in my beauty routine before I can go to sleep tonight."

"Sleep!" I shouted, pointing toward the bed and coming back into focus. "*That* is what beds are for."

Violet shifted her weight and rolled her eyes again.

"Beds are for sleeping," I continued. "NOT for jumping on, NOT for food fights, NOT—" I glared at my ten-year-old son—"for tying your sisters to the post."

"We were playing kidnappers," said Scoot, defending his honor. "I let them go when you paid me with the bag of Cheetos for ransom, didn't I?"

I held up my hand. "Sleeping in beds is a correct principle. It will help you all your life if you choose to follow it."

"What's a pimple?" asked Moo, sending his siblings into fits of laughter.

"*Principle!* It's a *principle*," I said, scooping him up into my arms. "I'm teaching you what to do with your bed. Do you think you can do it?"

He nodded, his chubby cheeks wiggling like jelly.

"Okay, children," I shouted, putting Moo down and clapping my hands for attention. "I have taught you what to do. When you go to bed, you must sleep. Your feet must never touch the floor. Now you must govern yourselves. It's time for bed. Ready, set, GO!" I folded my arms and closed my eyes triumphantly, waiting for the promised miracle.

The children all stared at each other and didn't move.

"Ahem," I cleared my throat.

"I've got to take a shower," said Violet. She stomped toward my bedroom.

"I'm going to make a toasted cheese sandwich," said Scoot, turning toward the kitchen. Then, seeing my glare, he said, "Just kidding. I'm going to bed. Hey, guys, get in your beds. I've got this great idea for a tightrope. We can tie all our blankets and sheets together and visit each other in our rooms."

The other children all cheered and ran to their rooms. "Beds are for sleeping," I called after them, reinforcing the principle. They couldn't hear me in the midst of tearing all the sheets off their beds.

"This is going to be awesome," said Scoot, beginning to unmake his bed.

"Ahem," I said, clearing my throat, folding my arms, and tapping my foot. "Beds are for *sleeping*," I said.

"What?" said Scoot. "I'm following correct principles. You said our feet couldn't touch the floor."

Later that night, my husband came home from basketball with his buddies to find me in bed with a pillow over my head.

"Honey," he said, lifting up a corner of the pillow. "Why are the kids playing checkers in the bathtub? When I asked them why they weren't in bed, they told me their feet never touched the floor." He paused, staring. "And what are you doing under this pillow? What are those noises you were making?"

"They're 'ohms'" I said. "I learned them in my yoga class. I'm trying not to hear the kids while they govern themselves."

My husband stared at me for a moment and then let the pillow drop back unto my face. Minutes later, I heard the squeals as my husband chased the kids back to their beds.

I shook my head. *Ah, well,* I sighed, governing myself with one of the first correct principles of marriage: hiding under the covers while your husband does all the dirty work. *At least I knew how to govern myself.* I smiled and shifted to get more comfortable in my bed. Thank goodness for correct principles.

26

Reach for the Stars

REALITY IS A NEBULOUS THING TO SOME PEOPLE, MOST PARTICULARLY TO dreamy teenage girls who have always known they were destined for greatness. I found this out one day while eavesdropping on my teenage daughter Violet's conversation with her cousin at a college basketball game. (Not that I would ever stoop to eavesdropping on my daughter; I just happened to overhear something as I was *stooping* to pick up something I *dropped* in the *eaves* of the stands, which is why I call it eavesdropping. Sheesh! What kind of mother do you think I am?)

"So," said Egbert, Violet's fourteen-year-old cousin and closest friend, "where are you thinking of going to college? Are you going to stick around here and live with your parents?"

Violet smiled lazily as she sipped her soda pop. "Probably not," she said. "I'll have to go wherever I can get a scholarship."

Good girl, I thought, leaning down closer to the two cousins so as to hear better while I searched.

"You're going to have to study hard and get straight As if you want a scholarship to BYU," said Egbert. "My mother always lectures me about that."

Violet laughed. "Study? Oh, I won't be doing any of that."

I choked on the piece of gum I'd been chewing, and my search halted. The two cousins looked behind them to see what was wrong with me. I smiled and pretended to keep coughing so they would continue on with their conversation.

Egbert's eyebrows pinched together. "What kind of a scholarship are you going to get if you don't study?" he asked.

Both cousins stood up and cheered as our team made a basket.

When the crowd settled back down, Violet leaned over to Egbert and said, "Basketball scholarship. I told you I was going to play in the WNBA someday, didn't I?"

Behind the cousins, my jaw dropped involuntarily and the gum fell out. Oops. Now I really was searching for something.

Egbert looked thoughtful. "Well, yeah, but have you ever played basketball? On a team? In your lifetime?"

Violet shrugged and flicked her straw so little droplets of pop flew into the air. "No, but how hard could it be?"

We all found out how hard it could be two weeks later at Violet's first school basketball game. She had decided, after Egbert had hyper-ventilated from laughing so hard, that it might be wise to get some experience on the middle school team before making any concrete plans for the future.

"Honey," I said, leaning toward my husband in the stands and pointing at Violet dribbling down the lane. "Aren't you supposed to only have one hand on the ball when you dribble?"

My children all covered their ears as the referee's whistle shrieked.

"Yep," said my husband.

Violet's teammates groaned as the other team got the ball. But Violet was no quitter. She used her quick wits and shifted over to defensive mode. We watched as she glued herself to the girl who had possession of the ball, literally, by draping herself behind the girl so closely, their ponytail holders entwined and got stuck together.

The referee's whistle shrieked again.

"Hey," yelled my husband. "There's no ponytail fouls in basketball."

Violet sent a glare in our direction as the two referees tried to untangle the girls' hair.

A few minutes later, Violet and her teammates lined up at the key while the other girl prepared to take her free-throw shot.

"No, no," said my husband under his breath. "She's lined up in the wrong spot." He bit his fist, trying to control his urge to coach his daughter from the bleachers.

There was some chuckling in the stands as Violet's coach tried to tell her to move to the right position, and she moved into the other wrong spot. But the real show was just beginning, and it wasn't on the floor of the gym.

My three-year-old son, Moo, the family showman, sensed his opportunity in the quiet moments before the girl at the free-throw line got ready to shoot.

"LET THE WILD RUMPUS START!" he boomed into the silence in his circus ringmaster voice, raising his finger into the air.

All eyes turned toward my family in the stands. Birdie was doing flips over the bar that divided the steps on the bleachers, and my other children were having slide races in their socks up and down some empty bleacher rows, much to the chagrin of the people sitting above them.

I elbowed my husband. "I thought you were watching the kids," I hissed.

"I thought *you* were," he replied, biting his fingernails and not taking his eyes off the game.

Sighing, I went over to lasso my kids back into their own bleacher seats. When I finally returned, my husband was smiling.

"What?" I asked him. "What happened while I was gone?"

My husband beamed at me. "That coach is brilliant," he declared. "He's discovered the one seed of sports talent passed down the Campbell line from generation to generation."

"What's that?" I asked, squinting toward the basket on the opposite end of the gym in order to see my daughter.

"Big feet."

My eyes widened. I stood up so I could see better. It was true. The coach had planted my daughter right next to the basket, where her big feet were tripping up all opposing team members within her vicinity.

Well, what do you know? Maybe Violet did have some basketball potential. The way those middle school girls were falling to the floor next to her left and right *was* pretty amazing. Any future WNBA scout would be bound to be impressed. Who was I to take away her dreams and bring her back to reality? Just remind me to never let her become an investment banker.

27

Cheaters Never Prosper

"THANKS TO YOU, I'M FINALLY GETTING INTO A ROUTINE," I TOLD MY FRIEND April one day as she sat at my kitchen table, rubbing her hands with hand sanitizer. After several failed attempts to avoid the terrors of unidentified microorganisms on previous visits, she had successfully made it to the table without touching anything or anyone. The hand sanitizer was just an extra precaution.

"I really think I've got this cleaning thing down," I told her. "That new card system you gave me is really working! Every morning, I just take out the cards and they tell me what to clean. Today was kitchen day. Just look at that shiny sink over there."

"Wow!" said April, getting up to admire the sink. "I don't think I've ever seen your sink before. It's always been full of dishes."

I grinned. "See? I've turned over a new leaf. Now you can visit me germ-free any time."

April laughed. "Well, I have to admit, I'm amazed. You've changed your whole outlook on life in the space of one week. How did you do it?"

There was a muted crash from underneath the sink. I stuck my foot in front of the cupboard door. "Oh you know me," I said. "I'm always trying to improve myself."

Just then, Hazel came marching into the kitchen, holding on to a long string with a small loop at the end of it.

She stopped to catch her breath. "I'm taking my bunny for a walk, Mommy."

I lifted one eyebrow.

"Bunny?" said April. "I didn't know you had a bunny."

"Neither did I," I mumbled, gingerly taking my foot away from the cupboard door and walking over to inspect the loop at the end of her string. It was holding on tight to a ferocious-looking dust bunny, with ears that my daughter must have fashioned with her own little hands. I stepped on it.

"Hey!" yelled my daughter. "You're stepping on Gus!"

I straightened and smiled at April. "Gus is her imaginary friend. We're always accidentally stepping on him." Then I shooed my daughter toward the living room and hissed into her ear. "Go take Gus to your room, dear. I'm sure he wants to play Chutes and Ladders or something."

She stood firm and folded her arms. "Dust bunnies can't play games. They don't have arms."

I heard a pop. April had reopened the top to her sanitizer bottle.

I laughed nervously. "Why, whatever are you talking about?" I asked, in April's direction. "We don't have dust bunnies in our home. We cleaned all those up last week, *remember?*" I put my arm around my daughter, surreptitiously shoving her sideways into the living room.

She skirted out of my arms and moved toward the kitchen table. "I made him out of the dust bunnies under my bed," she told April. "Mom said we couldn't have a real bunny."

April was clutching her throat as my daughter closed in.

"I even gave him a tail, see?" She picked up the dust bunny and held it close to April's nose.

April started to hyperventilate. She stood up slowly and edged away from my daughter. "Um," she said, "I have to go now. I forgot, I have to take a book back to the library." She grabbed her bottle of hand sanitizer and held it in front of her, as if to ward off evil.

Suddenly, there was a thunderous crash as the cupboard door

underneath the sink burst open and spewed forth a pile of dirty dishes.

April screamed.

I covered my face with my hands.

"Okay! Okay!" I wailed. "I cheated. I haven't been doing the card system. When I heard you at the door this morning, I stuffed the dirty dishes under the sink."

April stared.

"I couldn't do it," I said. "There was no spontaneity left in life. I felt enslaved to a deck of index cards. I started sweeping everything under beds and into closets, just to get the cards out of my pile. I pretended to lose index cards all over the house. I even hid them in the cat food." I sighed and looked down at my shoes. "I'm sorry. I've failed you. Now you'll never come and visit me again."

April moved toward me, taking a wide berth around my grubby son. "Don't worry," she said. "You don't need to change for me. I love you just the way you are.

"Besides," she continued, holding up her empty bottle of hand sanitizer. "I've got plenty more where this came from."

I smiled. "You're a true friend," I said.

April made her way toward the door, carefully picking her coat off the leather chair she had previously wiped with a sanitizing cloth. "True friends wouldn't let a dust bunny come between them," she said, sliding on her coat.

"Then you want to pet Gus?" asked my daughter, holding her little ball of dust in front of her face as she moved toward April.

"Don't push it," said April, backing out the door.

Suddenly my daughter stooped down, grabbing something from underneath the leather chair. "Hey, Mom! Here's one of those index cards you lost. It says to clean out your bedroom closet."

I took the card and stuffed it into the pocket of my jeans. "Don't worry. I've already done that," I said. "I swept everything under the bed with the dust bunnies."

28

Ecstatic Tidings of Enormous Joy

"MOM, WHATCHYA DOIN'?" ASKED MY PRESCHOOLER, ONE DAY, WHEN SHE FOUND me sitting at the kitchen table in front of a heap of crumpled-up papers.

"Argh!" I replied, crumpling up another piece of paper and throwing it over my shoulder. "I just can't get the right word." I tapped my head with my pencil. I looked over at my husband, who was fixing the drain underneath the kitchen sink. "Honey, what's another word for *famous*?"

"*Remarkable*," yelled my husband from deep within the bowels of the kitchen cupboards.

I shook my head. "No, maybe *distinguished*," I said.

"*Superstar*?" said my teenager from across the room.

"That's a good one," I said. Still it wasn't quite right. Frowning, I tapped my pencil on my chin. Then suddenly, I smiled. "Wait, no. I've got it!" I cried, stabbing my pencil in the air and knocking my daughter to the ground with my elbow. "*Legendary!*"

My daughter started to wail, "Daddy! Mommy knocked me down!"

My teenager sauntered over from where she'd been eating an orange. "Never stand too close to Mom when she's writing the family Christmas letter," she said, picking up my preschooler. "It could be dangerous."

"Ouch!" my husband said, bumping his head as he wormed his way out from underneath the sink. "Legendary? Who is legendary?"

"Our son," I said, smiling proudly. "Didn't you know that he's legendary with the teachers and the students in the band because he's the only one who can play two instruments?"

My husband looked confused. "Two instruments? I didn't even know he was in the band."

"Well, he's not *in* the band. It's just that all the band members wish they could be like him and do what he does."

"What does he do?" asked my husband, scratching his head with his wrench.

"Plays two instruments, like I said. He can play a duet with himself holding a recorder in each nostril. Now *that's* talent."

My husband's jaw dropped, and his wrench fell on his toe. "Talent? Legendary?" He held his injured toe and hopped around on one foot. "I can't *believe* I let you send this letter out every year," he said. "Our son is not famous—he's infamous. How can you put that he is *legendary* in band when he's not even in the band?"

I snorted. "Well, I'm certainly not going to put that he loves to gross out his friends by playing instruments in his nose."

My husband ran his fingers through his hair and began to pace the kitchen floor. "You see? This is exactly why I hate Christmas letters, from us or anyone else. It's just a bunch of braggy baloney that people send to each other so that they can look good in front of their friends."

I patted my husband's knee when he hopped by. "It's not that bad," I said. "Besides, a small amount of exaggeration in the family Christmas letter is expected. I mean, who writes what their family is really like? What kind of a world would that be?"

"An honest one," snorted my teenager, squirting orange juice in my face as she bit into her orange.

I shook my head and wiped the juice off my cheek. "You guys just don't understand. There's a code. It's called the Christmas code. You have to learn to decipher it."

I dug through my pile of papers. "Take this letter from Aunt Agnes.

She says her son broke his leg in a death-defying ski jump competition."

"Poor guy," said my husband.

"No, no, no!" I shouted, waving the letter in the air. "You have to translate the code. What she didn't say that he was skiing in the living room on a hill made of couch cushions, using his little sisters as skis."

My two daughters laughed and my husband's eyes narrowed. "How do you know that?" he said.

I puffed out my chest. "Years and years of deciphering Christmas letter code. People do the same thing with our letters. They spend hours and hours trying to crack our Christmas letter code to determine what really happened to our family this year. Would you take away all of their fun by writing what really happened?"

My husband rubbed his forehead, pondering. "But what if they get the code wrong?" he asked. "What if you write that our daughter loves to mountain climb, and they take it to mean that she climbs the bookshelf and hurls books at all her siblings as they walk by?"

I felt my eyes begin to gleam. "Mountain climbing. That's the perfect way to describe how she gets into her bed after not cleaning her room for a whole year!"

"Argh!" my husband gasped. He threw his hands up in the air and retreated back underneath his sink. I smiled. It was better this way. Leave the Christmas code writing to the expert. By the way, do you know another word for *social outcast*? I've got to find another way to describe my preschooler's habit of picking her nose in public.

29

Eels on Wheels

I TRY HARD TO BE AN EXAMPLE TO OTHERS. AND SOMETIMES, DESPITE THE FACT that my library fines exceed the national debt and I regifted my best friend's Christmas carrot cake last year, I'm even a good one. This is why I decided to invite my mother to go with me when I signed up to take meals to the elderly. I thought I might show her the great and marvelous things I do to help and lift people in need, and I also hoped it would erase the memory of the last time I tried to be an example by fixing her expensive venetian blinds so they no longer went up and down.

"Don't worry," I told my mother as I loaded all the meals in the car. "It won't take more than a half an hour. I've done this hundreds of times. I'm a pro by now."

"Yeah. And she's not going to send any old ladies into diabetic comas either by mixing up the desserts like she did last time," said my teenage daughter, who had been recruited along with the other kids to help out.

My mother's eyebrows shot up.

"She's exaggerating," I said. "It wasn't a coma. It was just a little bit of insulin shock, that's all. Nothing that couldn't be remedied with a piece of hard candy."

My mother cleared her throat nervously.

"Relax," I said, shooting my daughter a warning look. "Really. Things are going to be just fine. I know what I'm doing."

My mother nodded but sat stiffly in her chair. She didn't believe a word I said. She had raised me and knew what kind of trouble I could be to society at large when I decided to be helpful.

I set out to prove her wrong.

The first four deliveries went smoothly. The kids fought over which one of them got to carry what as we all stampeded toward the homes of the elderly.

"Just leave it on the porch," said one lady, who took one look at the pandemonium coming toward her house with bowls of spaghetti and refused to open the door.

"Mind the flowers," snapped another, fending my son away from her perennial beds with her cane.

My mother chose to watch from the car. She said she didn't want to add to the confusion.

I tried to explain that there was no confusion when suddenly I got confused. We were ready to deliver to the fifth house, and I noticed we were out of wheat bread.

"Oh no," I moaned. "This always happens. I gave the last lady wheat when I was supposed to give her white."

"Can white bread trigger diabetic comas?" my daughter asked my mother, tapping her on the shoulder.

"Hush," I snapped. "I need to think for a minute."

"Last time you just had the little kids take it to the door, so she would be distracted by their cuteness and not look at the color of the bread," said my son.

"Oh, I did not," I said. "I'm sure I just explained the situation to her."

"Yeah," said my eight-year-old, explaining to her grandma. "That's because we believe in being honest, true, and chased by an elephant."

My mother gave me a bewildered stare.

"She means chaste and benevolent, not chased by an elephant," I huffed. "Okay, look," I continued, chewing my nails, "maybe she won't care about the bread. Let's just take it to the door." I loaded everything but the bowl of spaghetti into the hands of my two youngest children.

"Try to look as sweet and adorable as you can," I whispered, shoving them down the sidewalk.

My mother rolled her eyes and put her hand to her forehead.

"It can't hurt," I said, shrugging. Unfortunately, my shrug was a little too enthusiastic, and I shrugged the bowl of spaghetti right into the juniper bushes.

I heard a groan from where my mother was sitting.

"No worries," I called, reaching down to grab it. "It's still covered. Oo. Ouch. These bushes are prickly."

I smiled at my mother. She sank lower into her seat.

"Aha! I've got it!" I cried, lifting it from the place where it had become wedged. But as I pulled it free, it was knocked from my hand by another prickly branch. It flew toward the street in what seemed like slow motion, and then, landing on its side, it began rolling down the hill.

"Noooooooooo!" I yelled, running after it.

"On top of spaghetti . . . ," my children sang at the top of their voices, "all covered with cheese." They collapsed into giggles.

"A little help, please?" I hollered, scrambling after the wayward bowl. No one came. They were too incapacitated by laughter. I saw someone peering out of the curtains of the front window of the house we were supposed to deliver to as I sprinted past.

"Tell her I'll be right there with the spaghetti," I yelled at my youngest children, who were still edging toward the door.

I madly chased the bowl, yelling insults at it, as it tumbled down the steep hill until finally, it collided with the tire of a confused motorist who had slammed on his brakes to avoid running over the crazy lady hollering and chasing a bowl of spaghetti.

"Doesn't look much like spaghetti anymore," said my son, eyeing the remaining contents of the bowl, when I returned to the car. "Looks like a pile of eels."

"Eels," I said, between wheezes, clutching my stomach. "We could try to pass it off as Japanese cuisine."

"Oh, honestly," snorted my mother.

"Yeah, except she might break her teeth on the rocks," yelled my teenager from the backseat. "And you can't fix that with hard candy."

I looked at the sweet elderly lady, giving me puzzled looks as she tried to keep my youngest son from playing with the rocks in her Zen garden with her cane.

"You like turkey and swiss?" I called to the woman, showing my mother that if honesty doesn't work, at least I could be benevolent. "I know a great sandwich shop just down the street."

"That'd be fine, dear," she said, "as long as it's on wheat bread."

"Wheat bread," I muttered to myself as I stumbled back into the car. "I'll give you wheat bread." I looked over toward my mother, who was chuckling to herself.

"What?" I said. "She says she likes turkey."

My mother continued laughing as she maneuvered the rearview mirror in my direction. "It's not that." Then she pointed to my head. "It's just—you might want to comb your hair before you come back," she said. "You look like you've been chased by an elephant."

30

Oh, Christmas Tree

ONE OF MY FAVORITE FAMILY TRADITIONS AT CHRISTMASTIME IS THE ANNUAL decorating of the tree. The lights, tinsel, music, and fistfight over whether the tree will be skinny or fat, all create within me a special feeling of warmth that causes me to tear up and have a catch in my throat. Of course, the throat problem could be caused by the fact that my vocal chords are strained from bellowing out too many orders. I admit, I love the fact that I get to be the general in charge of the whole crazy production, and I do perhaps tend to enjoy my glamorous image as Christmas CEO a little too much. That is why I was particularly disturbed when certain other members of my family somehow developed the mistaken idea that they were in charge.

"Okay, people!" I shouted into my toddler's toy microphone. "Line up and prepare to receive your decorating assignments. This year, I've made maps, graphs, and charts, so no one will be confused by my instructions."

Violet snickered. "Oh, you mean like last year, when you said we could only use recycled ornaments, and genius here"—she pointed to her younger brother—"came up with the most disgusting Christmas decoration yet known to mankind?"

My son gave his sister a shove. "What do mean? My dirty-sock Christmas tree was brilliant. A whole Christmas tree made out of dirty socks! Not only did it save water from not having to wash them, but it also cleaned up my room at the same time."

"Enough!" I bellowed into the toy microphone. "This is the season of love and giving. Now get over here and start decorating."

As the children scattered in every direction, melting into chaos, my husband cleared his throat. "We can't start decorating the tree yet, oh, Christmas One. The top of the tree is bent. It's too tall for this room. I think we should move it down to the basement where there's a higher ceiling."

I raised one eyebrow at him. "Are you deviating from the plan?" I asked, holding up a fistful of graph paper. "I stayed up all night, graphing where to put the lights in the yard, charting the most advantageous location of the tree, *and . . . and now you want to move it*?" I tried to give him my most daunting stare.

He stared back at me. "I let you have the skinny tree, so I get to decide where to put it."

"Humph," I replied, folding my arms. "What if I like the bent Christmas tree look? Who wants to have a perfect-looking Christmas tree anyway? What kind of a lesson does that teach our children? What about all the other poor little scrawny trees? How do you think they'll feel being passed by every year by our descendants?" I shook my head.

My husband rolled his eyes.

I shook my head. "No, a bent Christmas tree is definitely part of the plan this year, and we are not deviating from the plan."

My husband opened his mouth to argue but was interrupted when a yowling cat, tangled in Christmas tree lights, went streaking by.

"Here, kitty, kitty. Come back! We didn't get to plug you in yet," yelled Hazel, running past, two seconds later.

I held up my toy microphone. "I don't recall 'lighting up the cat' being part of my written instructions," I called after her.

Just then, Moo came bounding into the room with his blankie tied around his neck like a cape. "Don't worry, kitty. I'll save you." He chased his sister with a string of garland, swinging it like a lasso. "I've got something to tie her up with."

"No, no, no!" I cried into the microphone, getting an ear-piercing feedback sound when I tried to turn up the volume. "You're deviating from the plan. The garland is for the tree."

"Oh, let him have it," said Violet, stalking into the living room. "That garland is the ugliest decoration I've ever seen. Every year our tree looks the same—like a Christmas box exploded all over it. This year, I'm in charge of the tree."

"But . . . but . . . " I held up my Christmas tree chart. She waved my chart out of the way and started to dump the contents of the Christmas tree box all over the floor.

"Hey," I said, "some of those things are breakable you know."

"Okay, here," she said, handing me a fistful of candy canes. "I'm putting you in charge of the breakables. Hang these on the tree. They'll come in handy when I need a snack."

I looked over at my husband, who had a smirk on his face.

"She's so bossy," I whispered. "I don't know where she gets it from."

"I'm only hanging up things that go along with my theme," she said, holding up a shiny silver bell and making a face.

I looked over at my husband, who was laughing. I glared. "*Your* theme?" I said. "What's your theme?"

She smiled. "My theme is 'Your Oldest Daughter: Throughout the Ages.' I'm going to hang up any ornament that I've ever made or liked. It'll be sort of a Christmas tribute, to remind you of me."

I looked at my husband.

"I don't know where she gets it," he said, shrugging his shoulders.

Suddenly my ten-year-old son appeared, walking into the room with a great big grin. "Hey, everyone! What do you think of my new creation?" He held up a long grayish rope of socks, all knotted together. "It's a dirty sock *garland*," he said. "Much better than the dirty sock Christmas tree because you can use more socks."

"Ugh!" screeched my teenager. "That is so disgusting! Besides, it doesn't go along with my theme." She plugged her nose. "And it smells!"

"They're your dirty socks," said my son, holding them up. "I found them under your bed."

"Oh," said my daughter. "Well, if they smell like me, then that's a different story. That fits in with my theme. Bring them over here."

I sighed and threw my graph paper in the air. So much for this year's plan and being in charge. Anyway, I had to admit, my daughter was pretty good at being a Christmas tree CEO. At least she had the bossiness down right. Gingerly, I plugged my nose and walked past the bent tree, now covered in candy canes and dirty socks. I just hoped we could stand her taste in decor.

31

The World's Most Difficult Science

COLLEGE PROFESSORS MIGHT ARGUE THAT, IN ALL OF ACADEMIA, THE MOST difficult subject to comprehend and master is quantum physics. I disagree. I know for a fact, from years of experience, that the most difficult subject in the world to teach another human being is dental hygiene. I know this because, in spite of immersing my five little human beings in this subject for at least thirteen years, they have yet to comprehend it. Though they can master incredible feats of engineering, such as building giant slings the size of our swing set in order to fling apples at the neighbor kids, and negotiate complex, high-powered contracts for later bedtimes, the science of tooth decay (or the prevention thereof) remains an enigma to them.

The dentist thinks of our family as an exciting challenge. "It's always quite an adventure to clean your children's teeth, Mrs. Campbell. It's like fishing in an old pond. You never know what you're going to find—a rusty nail, someone's lost quarter, an old shoe . . . Maybe next time I'll pull up a used tire."

It's not that I haven't tried to teach them how to clean their teeth. Almost from their births, I have lined them up in my bedroom every morning and every night and asked them the same question: "Children, have you brushed your teeth?"

Every morning and every night, they give me the same answer, nodding like little angels.

"I don't know what that silly old dentist was talking about," I said to the children one night after they all confessed to being perfect in their tooth brushing habits. "He must have been exaggerating when he said he always sees dollar signs in front of his pupils when we walk in."

My husband snorted from the living room. "That's because you've been asking them the wrong questions. Ask them if they've brushed their teeth . . . *this week.*"

I looked over at the children, who were giving me confused stares, except for Violet, who was glaring at me as if I had offended her personal honor. "Of course!" she said. "Why would you even ask that question? We did it last Saturday."

I gave my husband a weary look as he entered the bedroom.

"They must be brushing their teeth," I said. "I have been replacing tubes of toothpaste like there's no tomorrow."

"Hmmm," said my husband as he marched down the line of children and inspected their teeth and gums. "Saturday, huh?" he asked our littlest one.

Moo grinned and nodded.

"And you used toothpaste?" asked my husband.

"Yep!" said our little boy. "My friend's puppy really needed a bath, so we used some to clean him up. That stuff smells really good."

"Tastes good too!" said Hazel.

I slapped my hand to my forehead. "Kids! How many times have I told you not to eat the toothpaste?"

Birdie said, "Don't worry, Mom. I stopped them before they could use it to draw pictures on the wall. I knew you wouldn't like it."

"Well, thank goodness for that," I said.

"Instead, I made them do it where you wouldn't have to see it, on the sidewalk in front of the Bankses' house."

I slumped onto the edge of my bed. My husband patted my shoulder.

"Honey, you don't have to worry," he said. "I have the solution." He walked over to his dresser and grabbed a bag. Then he reached inside the bag and pulled out some colorful automatic toothbrushes, shaped like famous movie characters.

The children cheered and ran to grab their favorite color.

"What? When did you get those?" I asked him.

"Today on my lunch break," he replied, "after you told me what happened at the dentist." He smiled. "I thought the kids could use a little extra incentive to brush more often."

"My hero," I sighed. "What would I ever do without you?"

My husband gave me a proud smile and raised his arms, puffing out his chest and flexing his muscles.

Just then, the cat flew by, yowling. It was followed a few seconds later by a stampede of squealing children with buzzing toothbrushes.

"Come back here, kitty! We just want to brush your hair," yelled our youngest son, tripping and trailing after the mob.

Then, our insightful Birdie came wandering back in to the bedroom, staring at her new toothbrush, which buzzed in endless circles, as if she had just solved one of the world's greatest mysteries. "I could use this to clean the sides of my fish bowl," she mused.

I looked over at my husband. His chest deflated.

"I guess I better start looking into some more dental insurance," he said.

"Yup," I said, patting his deflated chest muscles. "But don't worry. By the time all their teeth rot, I'll have taught them quantum physics. It's much easier than dental hygiene. Then they'll be rich. And they'll have to pay us back by taking care of us when we start losing our teeth."

32

Creativity Breeds Creativity

CREATIVITY IS AN EXCELLENT CHARACTER TRAIT TO CULTIVATE IN YOURSELF. In fact, most, if not all of my fulfillment as a mother comes from inventing new and exciting ways to foil my children's attempts to steal all of the bubble gum out of my purse. Why, without creativity, we would now be living without one of the most vital and important inventions of the twentieth century: cocktail wieners. Imagine a party without those!

The only time creativity becomes a problem is when you add *pro* in front of the word. This is because, somehow, during the procreative process, all of *your* precious creativity leaks out of you and seeps into your little creations. You think I'm making this up, but it's true. It's the only way I can explain why I get more spacey and less innovative and productive after each child is born. One by one, my children inherit all of my creativity and sap my inventiveness until finally, after five children, I am left with the ingenuity of a lima bean. This puts me at a decided disadvantage when my children use this pirated resourcefulness to sneak taco shells under each other's pillows at night or to trick me into paying them more allowance. And it starts to become really expensive when they invent couch cushion sleds to slide down the stairs.

The one bright spot in this dilemma is that the more creative your kids are, the better they will be able to support you in your old age. I tell my children this often, even up to eight times a day, because (1) I am not creative enough anymore to come up with any other method, and (2) they will be motivated to start training for a career when they are young.

This is possibly why my son Scoot has already zeroed in on a lucrative and exciting career as a computer hacker. He has already started his job training by cracking every computer and television code intended to keep him away from video games and junk TV.

I complained about this to my friend April one afternoon at the park.

"My son is going to jail by the time he's twelve—I just know it," I said, morosely pushing my toddler in the swing.

Always one to cheer and comfort, April doled out words intended to help me see reason. "Don't worry! They don't put twelve-year-olds in jail. They send them to juvenile delinquent homes. You've got plenty of time to turn him around."

I nodded. "Maybe you're right. I just get discouraged when I see other children who are so obedient. Look at that woman over there," I said, pointing at a woman pushing a stroller. "Why can't my son be like that child? His mother tells him to sit, and he sits. She tells him to eat vegetables, and he eats his vegetables."

April cleared her throat. "That's because he's six months old," she said. "He eats baby food. Strained peas are pretty good compared to rice cereal that tastes like cardboard. Besides," she whispered, "you've just got to use your wits. Outsmart the little devil into using his talents for noncriminal activities."

"That's easy for you to say," I wailed. "You've only got three children. You've still got some of your wits left."

April stared at me and pulled on her ear (something she does when she's trying to figure out what the heck I'm talking about).

I gave my toddler an underdog push and came over to where April was pushing her daughter. "What I mean is—I've tried everything.

There is no code my son can't crack. I'll think up the most obscure phone numbers or letter combinations, and within hours he's sitting in front of the television with all his siblings watching cartoons. He spends hours working out code-cracking algorithms in his bed. I've found notebooks filled with possible letter and word combinations. I'm telling you, he's brilliant. How am I supposed to raise a child when I can't protect him from himself?"

April patted me on the back and tried to put a positive spin on things. "Look on the bright side. If he turns into a criminal, maybe they'll make a movie about him someday . . . like Butch Cassidy and the Sundance Kid. Then he'll be famous!"

I raised an eyebrow.

"You're so lucky!" She smiled brightly. "My husband and I always wished we had a famous child. Why, when we were dating . . ." Suddenly she stopped. Her face lit up. "Wait a minute—that's it. I've got it!"

"Got what?" I asked, in moping tones.

"A code he'll never be able to figure out."

I raised my head, daring to hope. "Really? It's got to be simple enough for me to remember," I said.

She grinned. "You'll never forget this one. And he'll never figure it out." Then she dragged me over to a park bench. "Okay, listen," she said, sitting me down. "Your mistake is that you're using code words from the present—things that he knows about. You've got to go back to before he was born. We use this one on our computer. I can't believe I never thought to tell you about it."

She paused. My interest was piqued. "Well? Go on," I said.

"Nicknames," she said.

"Huh?" I said.

"You know." She flipped one side of her hair behind her shoulder. "Like the nicknames you and your husband called each other when you were dating. Your son wasn't around then. He'll never guess what you used to call each other."

I laughed. "You called each other nicknames? Like what? Poochie Woochie?

"Ha-ha," said April. "No. We only called each other respectable things, like 'Tiger' and 'Cowboy.'"

"Respectable." I nodded, swallowing my mirth. "Which one did your husband call you?"

April glared. "Very funny." Then a soft smile stole across her lips. "He used to call me Tiger because I growled at him a lot."

I tapped my chin with my finger, suddenly overcome with nostalgia for my own special nickname. "You know . . . you just might have something there. I bet my son would never guess what my husband used to call me in our more tender moments."

April smiled benevolently. "I love to hear these sweet stories. What did he call you?"

"Fatso," I said, staring up at the sky in fond remembrance.

April stared at me in horror. "What? He called you Fatso?"

I nodded. "He was studying Spanish, and he mistook the word *gordito* for a term of endearment. He didn't realize what the literal translation was." I shook my head. "I never did have the heart to tell him what it really meant."

April was quick to agree that my son would never be able to guess my old nickname. That night I had a chance to test out our theory.

I felt like a secret service agent as I closed all the curtains, checked for spy equipment, and felt around the lampshades for wiretaps before I told my husband what to type in the computer.

"He'll never guess what you used to call me." I chuckled, whispering the word to him in Spanish, just in case.

The next morning, my son called his little brother a name at breakfast. It was the Spanish word for "fatso."

"Argh!" I cried, slapping my forehead. "How did you guess the code? It hasn't even been in effect for twenty-four hours, and you weren't even alive at the time your dad called me that! What are you? Some sort of

ESP alien intelligence that stole my son from me at birth? Where is my son?" I said, shaking him by the shoulders. "Where has he gone, and what have you done with him?"

My son pushed me away and stared at me like I was nuts. Then he tapped his chin, like I always do when I'm thinking, clearly proving that he stole all his ingenuity from me. "Is that what the code was?" he said finally. "No wonder I couldn't crack it. Thanks, Mom! What a coincidence. I heard someone say that word in Spanish club yesterday. I think it's a term of endearment. I was using it on the baby. Babies like foreign languages."

It looked like my son had leeched some of his dad's intelligence as well. Oh well. Back to the drawing board for more obscure nicknames. Maybe I'd better start growling, so my husband can start calling me something more respectable and harder to figure out, like "Tiger."

33

Teenage Towers of Babel

ONE OF THE BIGGEST PROBLEMS BETWEEN TEENS AND PARENTS IS MISCOMMUNI-cation. This is because you and your teen no longer speak the same language. Gone are the days when you could blissfully tell your daughter "good morning," and she would say "good morning" back to you. Now, your innocent "good morning" is interpreted as, "You're late for breakfast, and your socks don't match. You've offended the family and all mankind with your heedless dressing."

Some people are puzzled by this phenomenon, but I have discovered the cause of this Tower-of-Babel-like curse. According to my extremely scientific and careful research of one teenager, I have conclusive evidence that at the exact minute your child turns thirteen, there is actually some sort of strange morphing phenomenon that starts to happen between what comes out of your mouth and what goes into your teen's ears. The curse descends upon your home and all its inhabitants and isn't lifted until seven years later. It's the only way I can explain the tearful out-bursts that happen every time I tell my daughter her hair looks nice. There are times when my words get so distorted that my daughter and I can no longer hold a coherent conversation. This is why one night, before dinner, I decided to take matters into my own hands.

"What are you doing?" said my husband, coming in one Saturday from cleaning out the garage.

I reached up to give him a kiss as I tied the last knot of my project and slid the meatballs out of his reach. "I'm making sandwich boards."

"Sandwich boards? What for?" he asked, snitching a meatball from a steaming platter.

"For improved communication in our family, especially with our teenager," I said, holding them up for him to see. "They tell whomever you are talking to what kind of mood you're in, so there can be no more misinterpretation of your intentions when you say things like, 'Have a nice day.'"

"Huh?" said my husband.

"Watch," I said, slipping one over his neck and turning it to the happy face side. "Tell me to have a nice day."

"What?" asked my husband.

"Just say it," I said.

"Okay. Okay. Have a nice day," he repeated.

"Thank you!" I smiled brightly. "I will, because I know you were happy when you said it. You showed me the happy face on your board. "

My husband gave me a pained look. "Have you been talking psychology with April again?"

I shook my head. "No, I haven't. I'll have you know I thought this one up myself."

My husband snorted.

I turned up my nose and gathered up my sandwich boards. "You just watch," I said. "It'll work."

I walked over to the top of the stairs and put a sandwich board around my neck. I turned it to the side with the happy face, grinning at my husband and pointing down at it.

My husband shook his head and snitched another meatball from the platter. I frowned, but he just grinned and pointed at the happy face on my chest.

Rolling my eyes, I cleared my throat, ready to test my experiment. I rolled up my sleeves and took a deep breath.

"Time for dinner," I whispered. Then, "Time for *dinner*. Time *for* dinner. No, no. *Time* for dinner. *Time for* dinner."

My husband came over to stand beside me, squinting at me as I talked. "What are you doing?"

I waved him away. "I'm practicing my nuances and inflections, so as not to offend," I said.

"Oh brother," he said, walking back over to the meatballs.

Finally, I had it right. I took another deep breath.

"TIME FOR DINNER," I called. I heard a bedroom door slam deep within the bowels of the basement.

Ten seconds later, Violet appeared at the bottom of the stairs. "Why do you always have to yell at me?" she said, stomping up the stairs.

"I wasn't yelling," I said. "I had to speak loudly so you could hear me." I flashed my smiley face sandwich board in her direction. She batted it out of the way and moved past me.

"Oh," she said. "Well, what's for dinner?"

"Meatballs and gravy," I answered, cheerfully. "You want to come help me . . ."

"Meatballs and gravy?" she squealed. "Ew! You made that because you hate me!"

"Huh?" I said.

"I know it! You made it just so that I would starve. You're trying to tell me I'm fat, aren't you?"

Frantically, I waved my smiley face at her. "We're not trying to starve you. That's ridiculous. We love you."

Her eyes narrowed and she pointed. "Oh, yeah? Then what's with the angry face? Huh? Are you trying to make fun of me? Don't you think I get enough of that at school? I can't believe you people!" She folded her arms, pursed her lips, and gave me the mightiest stink-eye that she could muster.

I lifted my sandwich board so I could look at it. "Angry? This is a happy face. See his mouth is a U shape. Happy." I held it out for her to see.

She glared. "That is angry. The mouth squiggles in the corner right there. And the eyes are squinty."

"Squinty?" I said. "How could they be squinty? They're just dots."

"Humph." She snatched the cat as it was walking by. "I'm going back to my room with the only one in this family who loves me." Then she whirled around and stomped back down the stairs. A few seconds later, we heard a door slam.

I looked over at my husband, who shrugged and snitched another meatball.

Rats. It looked like the morphing teen Tower of Babel curse extended to primitive stick-figure drawings too. Oh, well. Maybe I could develop some sort of happy sign language. But first, I'd have to exercise my fingers so they'd be limber enough to get all the right nuances and inflections.

34

The Budgeting Frontier

WHEN MONEY IS TIGHT, IT'S ALWAYS WISE TO LIVE ON A BUDGET. THAT'S WHY I never budget. I'm not that wise or that good at keeping track of numbers. But because I am creative and I do enjoy things such as eating and wearing clothes, I regularly come up with brilliant money management plans for the budget impaired. These amazing "no-work" plans for saving money are unlike any other moneymaking scheme or scam you've ever heard before. Plus, they are absolutely honest in their no-work guarantee. They almost never work. But one particular summer, I came up with a money management plan so fresh, so courageous, and so inventive, I knew it couldn't fail.

"Hey, Mom! Why are there Lincoln Logs taped all over our front door?" yelled my teenager from the front of the house, returning from swimming at the city pool with her friends.

"Yeah! Why *are* there Lincoln Logs taped to our front door? And why is it so hot in here?" asked my husband, who had picked her up from the pool after work.

I wiped my hands, which were sticky from biscuit making, on the makeshift apron I had made out of one of my husband's old dress shirts. Then I mopped the sweat from my brow. "It could be the fireplace. I just started a fire," I replied.

"Fire?" they both cried at the same time.

"Why in the world would you start a fire?" asked my husband. "It's summer! And it's one hundred degrees outside!"

I grinned. "It's pioneer day! My new idea! It's going to be so fun. The younger kids got excited and wanted to make our front door look like a log cabin. Besides . . . ," I said, "I used up all of our grocery money for the month. So I had to invent a new way to save money."

My husband groaned and put a fist to his forehead.

"I know what you're thinking," I said, raising my hand. "You're thinking, *Not another one of those money-saving plans that end up costing us a fortune.*"

My teenage daughter snickered.

"Well, don't worry," I said. "That was the old me, the half-committed me. This time I'm serious. Besides, this plan can't cost us any money."

"Why is that?" asked my husband, snitching some biscuit dough from the kitchen island.

I slapped his hand. "Because," I said, "I shut off all our electricity."

"You WHAT?" Violet and my husband both looked at me like I was out of my mind.

"I was touched by the pioneer spirit!"

"I'll say you were touched," said my daughter, "in the head."

Ignoring her, I went on. "Today I was thinking to myself, why save three cents by turning out a light, when you can quadruple your savings by living without electricity, just like the pioneers? Why spend all your time clipping coupons when you can live off the land for free? Those pioneers really knew a lot about saving money. Did you know they lived in houses made of mud? Think of the cost-effectiveness of that!" I said. "Home repair would be dirt cheap."

"Hey! Look!" interrupted Scoot, leaving mud prints as he walked across the kitchen floor. "Now you can't yell at me for getting the floor dirty. It's Pioneer Day. I'm helping establish some atmosphere."

"What have you been doing?" I cried. "Why are your shoes so muddy?"

He smiled and puffed out his chest. "I was trying to catch our dinner—just like a real pioneer manly-man."

"Catch our dinner?" asked my husband.

"Yeah," said my son, grinning grinned my son. "I guess I shouldn't have let the neighbor's rabbit out of its cage before I tried to get it with my BB gun. Those things are fast."

My husband choked. "You were hunting our neighbor's pet rabbit?"

My son pointed at me. "Mom said pioneers ate wild rabbits and deer."

"*Wild* rabbits, not tame ones," said my husband.

My son shrugged. Then he spotted the fire. "Cool! Can I burn some biscuit dough? Or what about this?" he asked, snatching my daughter's purse off the counter.

"Hmmm," I mused, "catching our own dinner would save us money—of course, I was thinking more of backyard chickens . . ."

"Backyard chickens?" my husband cried. "You can't have backyard chickens! There are city ordinances."

"Could we go back to the question of electricity?" interrupted my daughter, shoving her brother aside and grabbing her purse out of his hands. "How are you going to cook the food? What about showers? We won't have any hot water," she added, her voice rising in panic.

"It's true. Showers could pose a problem . . . with no running water," I said, tapping my chin with my finger.

"No running water?" cried everyone in the room except my son, who thought showers were highly overrated.

"What?" I said. "Pioneers didn't have faucets. Besides think of the money we'll save . . ."

"I'm running away," said Violet.

"No need," said my husband. "I'm going downstairs right now to turn the electricity back on." He marched away purposefully, telling our son to stop throwing napkins into the fire.

I glowered. Mutiny. I should have known. What happened to the true tough pioneer stock, like me? Where was my family's pioneer spirit? I bent over and took out a candy bar from my secret survival stash under the kitchen island. *Guess I won't be needing these anymore*, I thought, grumpily gnawing on a Snickers bar. I was planning on using chocolate to get me through the tough times when we would be living off goat's milk and wild berries. I frowned, thinking, *I didn't even get a chance to tell them about the dairy goats I was going to buy.* Then I stopped chewing. Wait a minute! That's it! Goats! We could sell the milk to gourmets like Harold and Hilary next door! Why buy gourmet goat's milk at the store when you can get it fresh from your neighbor's backyard?

Yes! The kids could learn to work by milking goats! We'd make millions! And making money was even better than saving it! I ran downstairs. I had to find my husband. He was going to love my new brilliant no-budget, no-work money management plan!

35

Waste Not, Want Not

IN MY EXPERIENCE, THE NUMBER ONE MOST VALUABLE AND ELUSIVE ENTITY IN A mother's life is time. After spending all day making dinner, chasing the neighbor's dog out of your tulips, wiping lipstick hieroglyphs off your baby's forehead, and scrubbing deodorant drawings off your walls, there is just not enough time left over for anything else. Because of this universal problem, thousands of studies have been performed and expert articles written on the subject of saving time. But I say the experts have missed the point. The real problem is that most women don't know how to waste time properly. If they knew how to procrastinate, become unproductive, and generally waste their time on things they wanted to, their need for saving time would be banished.

Possessing a large amount of natural talent in the underappreciated life skill of time wasting, and having become somewhat proficient in the subject through years of practicing and perfecting various wasteful techniques, I felt it my duty to perform my own expert study. I wanted to see if I could train the most notoriously productive and efficient person I knew how to save time—my way. It was Christmas morning, and my husband didn't even suspect the wonder and beauty of the gift he was about to receive.

"Honey! You shouldn't have!" said my husband after unwrapping the largest Christmas present under the tree. "You got me a . . . " He turned the giant box upside down and shook it. "It's a . . ." He looked at me.

I smiled. "It's a box!" I said.

"A box," he repeated, turning it back over and peering inside. "Why, thank you! You always know just what to get me. A big red box."

"This is not just any box!" I said, jumping to my feet in my excitement. "This is your new 'time-saving' box. It's going to give you back all the time you've been losing."

"My 'time-saving box.' How is a box supposed to save me time?"

I sighed and threw my hands in the air. "Have you no vision, man? Can you not see that this is the most ingenious, thrilling, time-saving invention ever to be known or used in the history of mankind?"

He raised his eyebrows. "Yeah? Who invented it?"

I let my hands drop and smiled demurely. "Why, me, of course. And you're the first one to be able to try it."

He cleared his throat. "Not to, uh . . . be ungrateful or anything . . . but what do you know about saving time?"

My eyes widened. "Are you kidding me? Do you ever notice me doing unnecessary tasks?"

He thought for a moment. "No, I guess not."

"And do you see me regularly reading books and lounging around in my pajamas?"

He nodded slowly.

"Well," I said, "where do you think all that extra time comes from? I'm telling you, I have a natural aptitude for finding extra time. I'm an expert! And I'm going to teach you everything I know. Follow me."

He looked worried, but he left the kids to play with their new presents and followed the box and me to the study.

"Now," I said, sitting him down in a swivel chair. "Getting more time out of each day is simple when you do things my way."

He looked dubious.

Ignoring the look, I went on. "The secret is procrastination and skipping steps."

He stood up. "Okay. That's it. I don't want to hear this—"

"No, wait!" I said. "See for yourself." I pointed to a stack of old coats, boots, and snow pants, which rose up out of its box and nearly reached the ceiling. "See that?"

He gulped.

"That is how I have saved hours of my life. Every spring, I throw the kid's snow gear in that pile. Then, resolving to clean it up before the next winter, I procrastinate and twiddle my thumbs all year until winter comes around again." I paused, waiting for the information to sink in. Getting no response, I continued, "The next year, when it comes time to drag out the winter clothes, I have forgotten where I put them, so I'm forced to go to the store and buy new coats.

My husband blinked at me. "And that is good because . . . ?"

I sighed. "BECAUSE! Can't you see?" I shook him by the shoulders and then pointed to the dangerously leaning coat tower. "Buying new coats only takes a fraction of the time it would to organize that monstrous pile."

He snorted.

Undeterred, I lifted the giant box onto his lap. "And THAT is what you're going to do with this box. You are going to toss in all the tasks and projects that you spend so much time on every day, and leave them for later."

He blinked at me, as if he didn't understand what I was saying.

"You know," I said, "Procrastinate the unnecessary so you can have more time for yourself."

He put his nose in the air. "Nothing I do is unnecessary." He picked up a stack of bills so that he could work on them while we talked.

"Right," I said, snatching the bills and throwing them in the box. "Now. I want you to practice what you are going to do while you have so much time on your hands. Go ahead."

He stared at me.

"Go on," I said.

"What?" he replied.

"Twiddle your thumbs and stare blankly at the ceiling, like this. Now don't worry if you're not as good as me, I've had years of practice. Just try it."

He blew out his breath and reached for the bills in the giant red box.

I snatched the box away, just in time. "Okay, okay," I said. "Cruise recipe sites on the Internet?" I asked. "Buy shoes online? Chat with your hunting buddy, Ernie, on the phone? Wait, I know!" I said, feeling magnanimous. "I'll let you work on my old junior high stamp collection."

I had to stop the suggestions when I noticed his face turning three shades of crimson.

"Fine," I said, backing slowly out of the room. "Take a nap if you want to. Just stay down here and waste time. I'm going upstairs to check on the kids, and I don't want to catch you doing anything important when I come back downstairs."

He stared at the wall. He was a quick learner.

Carefully I closed the door, not wanting to disturb his catatonic state, satisfied that my job was done.

Five seconds later, I heard noises coming from the room.

Throwing the door open, I said, "What are you doing? I thought I told you to stare at the ceiling, and here you are, organizing and ruining my coat pile."

He kept sorting furiously. He had slipped into his super-organized, time-saving efficiency mode. I'd seen it before in types like him. He could no longer see or hear me.

I sighed and closed the door. I guess some people would never develop a knack for time wasting. So much for my expert study. No matter. I could use my hard-won expertise to find clever ways to waste enough time for the both of us. Now there's something worth spending time on.

Afterword

The stories in this book are based on real events that have happened to our family, relatives, and friends. I liberally used my "humorist license" to exaggerate and add details to make the stories more fun, however. You can find more funny stories about our family in my first book, Confessions of a Completely (In)sane Mother, *and on the website www.authorkerstencampbell.com.*

FROM THE REAL-LIFE DIARY OF KERSTEN CAMPBELL:

Today, one of my favorite people in the world came up to me and said, "I wish I could be a mother more like you."

I stared at her and thought, *Ha! The idea is ludicrous! Does she realize that this morning we were twenty-five minutes late to school because the baby had taken a bottle of honey and squeezed it all over my son's left shoe? We would have used other shoes, but who could find them under the thousands of origami sculptures on the floor of his room?*

This woman is amazing. Many times I have wished to be just like her. I should write a book showing what life is really like inside every "perfect" home. My family and I are far from perfect, but I wouldn't have it any other way. Real joy in families is found in laughter at life's ups and downs and loving each other along the way.

About the Author

*"Ever wonder what your mother is really thinking?
Read her journals. They're very enlightening. Hope-
fully, you can handle finding out all mothers are
completely insane . . . But in a good way.
You'll see what I'm talking about."*

—Violet

Kersten Campbell is the author of the humor book *Confessions of a Completely (In)sane Mother* and more than thirty-five magazine and newspaper articles that support families, children, and motherhood. When not writing, she enjoys reading, painting, eating chocolate doughnuts, and playing the clarinet. She, her husband, five children, a cat, and a dog who is smarter than all of them live blissfully eating doughnuts in the state of Washington. (The dog steals most of the doughnuts.)

To read more of her humor stories and share some of your own, visit www.authorkerstencampbell.com.